# Lakeland's Easiest Walks

## Doug and Margaret Ratcliffe

**Published by** Sigma Leisure – an imprint of
Sigma Press, Stobart House, Pontyclerc, Penybanc Road
Ammanford, Carmarthenshire SA18 3HP

**British Library Cataloguing in Publication Data**

A CIP record for this book is available from the British Library

**ISBN:** 978-1-85058-848-1

**Typesetting and Design by:** Sigma Press, Ammanford, Carms

**Maps:** Doug Ratcliffe

**Photographs:** Doug and Margaret Ratcliffe

**Printed by:** Cromwell Press Group, Trowbridge, Wiltshire

**Disclaimer:** The information in this book is given in good faith and is believed to be correct at the time of publication. No responsibility is accepted by either the author or publisher for errors or omissions, or for any loss or injury howsoever caused. Only you can judge your own fitness, competence and experience.

# Preface

The Lake District and surrounding area has become far more accessible for wheelchairs and pushchairs in recent years. Most towns and villages are now well served with dropped-curbs and there are a few paths, for example at Grasmere and at Bowness, which have been adapted especially for wheelchair use.

Some of the paths described in this book are steeper and have rougher surfaces than others, but all of them should be accessible for pushchairs and at least partially accessible for manual wheelchair users. It can't be stressed too strongly that the suitability of any path for people with limited mobility depends not only on the type of wheelchair being used (manual, powered, or mobility scooter), but also on the physical fitness of both the wheelchair user and of his or her carer. If you find you're having difficulty on any of the walks, turn back straight away. I've completed all of these walks using a standard powered wheelchair without difficulty but know for a fact that I would need to turn back in a few places if I was using my lightweight mobility scooter and I might need to turn back in my manual wheelchair, depending on who was pushing me. Potentially difficult sections are mentioned under "Path Quality" for each walk.

Although essentially a book for wheelchair users, the paths are equally suitable for young children and toddlers in pushchairs. With this in mind the location of children's playgrounds have been noted and marked on the maps.

Many of the entries also have a Points of Interest section describing features that can be seen from the paths and the photographs included illustrate the fact that a wheelchair or pushchair is no barrier to the wonderful Lakeland scenery. We hope that you enjoy the walks as much as we have.

Doug and Margaret Ratcliffe
October 2009

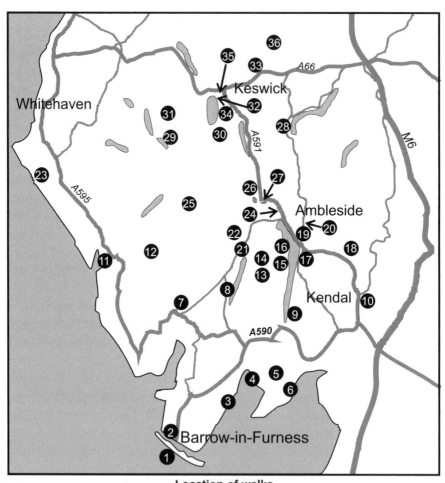

Whitehaven

Keswick

Ambleside

Kendal

Barrow-in-Furness

A66

M6

A591

A595

A590

**Location of walks**

# Contents

## The Walks

# Notes for Manual Wheelchair Users

We have listed the twelve walks below as those that are more suitable for manual wheelchair users who are either doing the walks alone or whose carers are not particularly strong or fit. Please note however that as everyone's circumstances and physical abilities are different the notes are intended for general guidance only, not as specific recommendations.

**Walk 1 Walney Island:** Level and suitable, especially the tarmac path to the North.

**Walk 2 Barrow-in Furness, Dock Museum:** Level, paved, and suitable.

**Walk 3 Ulverston, Canal Foot:** Level tarmac from Canal Foot along the canal towpath but then there is a short but steep slope up to the main road. If you can get up this the rest of the walk to the Lakes Glass Centre should present few problems.

**Walk 4 Haverthwaite:** Level tarmac as far as Roudsea Wood.

**Walk 6 Grange-over-Sands, Promenade:** There is a fairly gentle slope from the car park up a ramp onto the promenade. If you can manage this the promenade is level tarmac throughout. We would not recommend leaving the promenade to go through the ornamental gardens however as this would involve fairly short but steep gradients.

**Walk 10 Kendal, Riverside Walk:** The path from the car park along the riverside is level and, paved and should present few difficulties until roads have to be crossed. At these points traffic and some fairly gentle slopes make the walk rather more challenging.

**Walk 16 Windermere Lake, Red Nab:** A mainly level walk but the pebbly surface might present problems in places.

**Walk 21 Coniston:** The roadside path from Monk Coniston into Coniston itself should be fairly straightforward. We would not recommend the detour along the lakeshore however as this has a very poor surface in places. If you continue on through Coniston to the Coniston Boating Centre there is a short very steep and awkward footpath over the bridge just past the Church.

**Walk 24 Ambleside, Rothay Park:** The circular walk through Rothay Park is fairly level and mainly paved throughout. The bridge over the River Rothay is steep however and the road to the right has some fairly steep sections.

**Walk 26 Grasmere:** Virtually level and paved throughout.

**Walk 29 Buttermere:** The walk is level with a good surface as far as the lake but the lakeside path itself has some short fairly steep slopes and a more challenging surface in places.

**Walk 32 Keswick, Friar's Crag:** From the car park there is a fairly gentle slope on the road down to the lakeside path. This is virtually level with a reasonable surface as far as Friar's Crag. The rest of the walk is more difficult because there are gentle to moderate slopes over a fair proportion of its length.

# *Key to Maps*

*The sketch maps are not accurate and are intended simply to give an overview of the walks. They should be used in conjunction with the relevant Ordnance Survey Map.*

Path

Road

Track

River

Railway

Sea or Lake

Wood or Forest

**P** Car Park   **T** Disabled Toilet   **C** Children's Playground

*All the maps are orientated with North at the top of the page and all are drawn to different scales, as indicated on each map.*

# 1. Walney Island

| | |
|---|---|
| **Distance:** | 3¼ miles in total, there and back |
| **Summary:** | A low level coastal walk, typical of Walney Island with views back across the island towards the shipbuilding yards at Barrow-in-Furness |
| **Car parking:** | From Barrow-in-Furness cross the bridge onto Walney Island and basically carry on in a straight line until you reach Sandy Gap car park near the West coast of the island |
| **Disabled toilet:** | From the car park head back towards Barrow-in-Furness and turn left in front of the Golf Club. After about ½ mile take the second left, signposted 'West Shore Earnse Bay', into West Shore Road. In ¾ mile the disabled toilet is on the left by the car park |
| **Path quality:** | The path is level throughout and the surface varies from tarmac and concrete to rather bumpy loose pebbles in places |
| **Map:** | Ordnance Survey Explorer OL6 Grid reference: SD177682 |

## Directions

The path to the North of the car park (point B to point A) is a delight for wheelchair users. It is level tarmac throughout and feels to be virtually on the beach. (In actual fact it is about five yards away). It starts, to the right, at the end of the road by the beach.

The path to the South starts from the car park (point B to point C) and its surface varies from very good to rather bumpy in places.

**Tarmac path north of the car park**

It continues along the shoreline for about ¹/₄ miles before ending at another car park right on the shore (point C).

## Points of interest

Walney Island, at eleven miles long and nearly one mile wide is the eighth largest island off the English coast. It is a low-lying sandy island with salt marshes and two important nature reserves, one at each end if the island. It was joined to the mainland in 1908 by the construction of the Jubilee Bridge, and it's population increased dramatically in the early 20th century, to stand at approximately 13,000 today, with the building of Vickerstown to house the shipyard workers of Barrow-in-Furness.

Walney's reputation as one of the windiest shorelines in England has not gone unnoticed by the wind-farm developers. There is an offshore wind-farm to the west that does nothing to enhance the dramatic sunsets for which this area is famous.

**Looking from Walney Island towards the giant shipbuilding sheds
at Barrow-in-Furness**

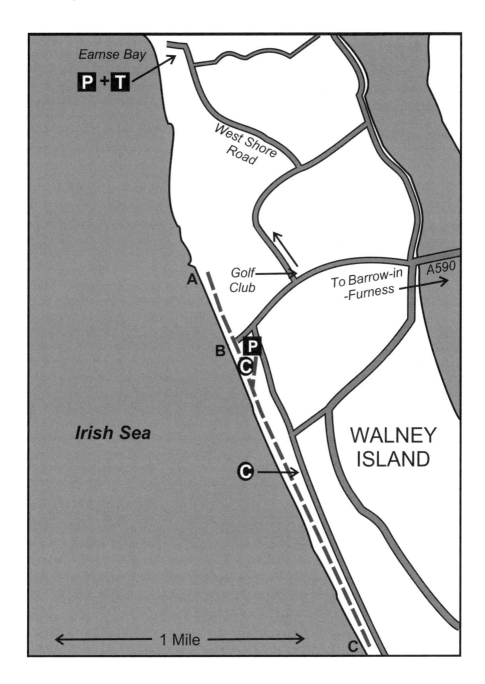

# 2. Barrow-In-Furness, Dock Museum

| | |
|---|---|
| **Distance:** | About 2 miles there and back |
| **Summary**: | A level paved walk along the shoreline together with an interesting free museum visit, which is fully accessible for wheelchair users |
| **Car parking:** | There is a small car park at the start of the walk (see Directions below). Alternatively there are 6 disabled parking spaces in front of the museum and a further 6 disabled spaces on the main museum car park |
| **Disabled Toilet:** | Inside the museum. NB: Museum is closed on Mondays in summer and on Mondays and Tuesdays in winter (November to March) |
| **Path quality:** | Level and paved |
| **Map**: | Ordnance Survey Explorer OL6 Grid reference: SD191692 |

## Directions

Coming from Walney Island the car park at the start of the walk is just over the bridge onto the mainland on the left directly opposite a modern office building called Waterside House.

The walk starts from the car park through a delightful small garden area called Channelside Haven, which is well worth exploring in its own right. Resuming the walk head for the masts of a small sailing club and take the path behind it, signposted 'W2W 20'. Where the path opens out into a large gravelled area with a water filled dock at the side you can either continue the walk by following the shoreline round to the left or alternatively bear right towards the Dock Museum. From the Dock

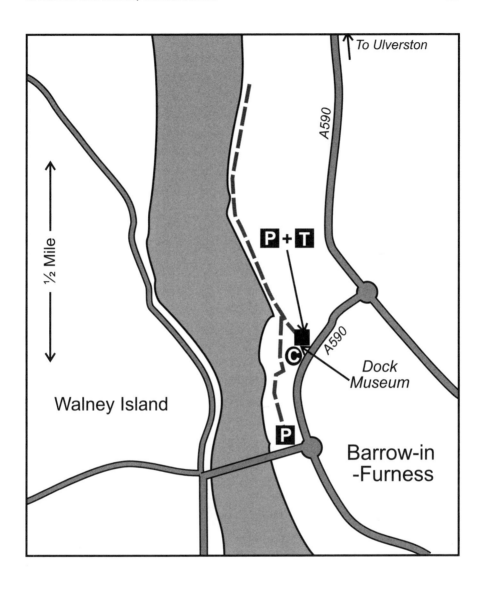

Museum the walk continues by going over a wooden footbridge and turning left along the side of the dock to continue on for another ²/₃ mile or so. Return is by the same route.

**The path from the Museum**

# Points of interest

The museum, established in 1897 as Barrow Museum, charts the social and industrial history of the region, with particular reference to the shipbuilding industry. The present building, opened in 1994, is built over an old dry dock.

Admission to the museum is free, and it is fully accessible for wheelchairs with a lift to all three floors. One thing that impressed me about this visit was the view out of the window on the lowest level, where it becomes apparent how big this old dock actually is.

**The Dock Museum, with the massive shipbuilding sheds behind**

# 3. Ulverston, Canal Foot

| | |
|---|---|
| **Distance:** | 2½ miles there and back |
| **Summary:** | Canal Foot has stunning views across the estuary and the canal has a mile-long level tarmac towpath, which serves also as a farm access road. There are pleasant views over open countryside |
| **Car parking:** | As you approach Ulverston from Newby Bridge on the A590 go straight on at the first round-about and then take the next left down North Lonsdale Road (Signposted 'South Cumbria Industrial Area, Canal Foot'). After about a mile turn left at the T-junction and continue on until you reach a small parking area by the shore |
| **Disabled toilet:** | 50 yards on from the car park on the left. RADAR key required. Also inside the Lakes Glass Centre |
| **Path quality:** | Level tarmac except for steep 5 yards slope at point A |
| **Map:** | Ordnance Survey Explorer OL7 Grid reference: SD313776 |

## Directions

The walk starts by crossing the bridge over a disused canal lock. If you carry straight on there is a short coastal road that, after about 50 yards passes the disabled toilet and continues on to provide access to a few bungalows. Returning to the bridge, turn right just before it to the canal towpath. There is a locked gate across the end of the towpath to restrict unauthorised vehicular access but with pedestrian access at the side wide enough for most wheelchairs and scooters. The canal continues straight for a good mile before reaching the main road at point A. There is a short (5 yards) fairly steep gradient up to the road. Turn right and follow the pavement round to the right at the two roundabouts and into the car park. You will see the Lakes Glass Centre across the car park from the supermarket. A door in the centre of the building leads to a small free display showing the history of Ulverston and if you turn right at the end of the corridor there is a public viewing area where you can watch the glassblowers at work.

## Points of interest

The Ulverston Canal is the shortest, straightest, deepest, widest canal in the country. It is 1½ miles long, 15 feet deep and 66 feet wide and was built in 1796 to enable ships to be loaded and unloaded right in the town itself. It was in use commercially throughout the whole of the nineteenth century and a passenger ferry used to sail from here to Liverpool and also to Fleetwood and Barrow-in-Furness. The canal suffered commercially by the opening of the Furness Railway in 1846. The Railway Company bought the Canal in 1862 and it continued to use it for

**Derelict lock gates on the Ulverston Canal**

**The Hoad Monument**

trade until 1916. Unusually the canal was sold to the railway company for a profit, unlike most other canals, which ended up being sold for a fraction of the cost of construction. In Ulverston's case the canal cost £9,000 to build in 1796 and it was sold for £22,000 in 1862.

The most noticeable landmark in Ulverston, the Hoad Monument was built on a hill overlooking the town in 1850 to commemorate Sir John Barrow who came from the town and who was a founder member of the Royal Geographical Society. The 100 foot high monument is a copy of the Eddystone lighthouse. It is known locally as 'the pepper pot' and it is so prominent that in the Second World War the Germans promised the people of Ulverston that they would bomb their pepper pot!

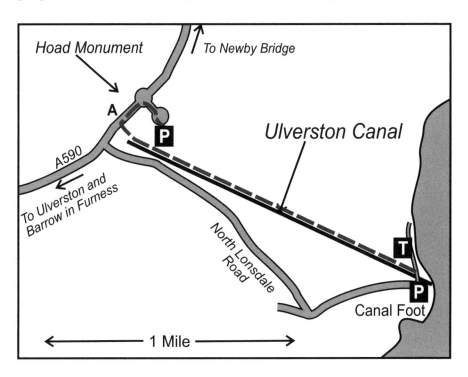

# 4. Haverthwaite

| | |
|---|---|
| **Distance:** | 3½ miles to point C, there and back |
| **Summary**: | A peaceful country stroll on the coastal plain of the Leven Estuary with riverside and woodland views. Mainly on virtually traffic-free level tarmac, this is a decent length walk to suit most abilities |
| **Car parking:** | Lay-by as you turn from the B5278 at point A |
| **Disabled toilet:** | On the platform at the Haverthwaite Railway Station. A RADAR key is needed and the toilet is only accessible when the station is open.If it is closed the nearest disabled toilet is 7 miles away at Ulverston Canal Foot (see Walk 3) |
| **Path quality:** | Level tarmac to point B and then gentle gradients with tarmac to point C and fairly good surfaces to point D |
| **Map**: | Ordnance Survey Explorer OL7 Grid reference: SD346836 |

## Directions

From the lay-by follow the lane away from the B5278. This quiet farm access lane continues across flat pasture land for about 1¼ miles before entering Roudsea Wood at point B. The woods to the left comprise the Roudsea Nature Reserve, accessible only by permit from English Nature. Continue through the woods until point C where a track on the right is signposted 'Route 20' with a blue National Cycle Network sign. This track leads out of the woods with long distance views of the village of Greenodd across the estuary. The track leads to a solitary house (point

**The River Leven from the path**

D) beyond which it is too rough for most wheelchairs and scooters. Return back to the car by the same route.

## Points of interest

Roudsea Wood and Mosses is an important National Nature Reserve and a Site of Special Scientific Interest. Having both limestone and slate sub-soils, it has a variety of different habitats for plants and animals. It has several species of rare plants, moths and butterflies. One species, the Rosy March Moth, which was believed to have been extinct in England since the 1850's was discovered here in August 2005.

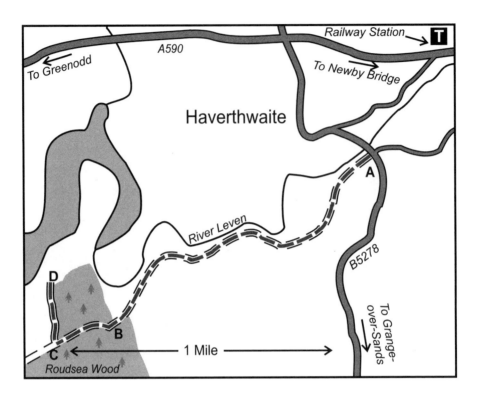

# 5. Cartmel

| | |
|---|---|
| **Distance:** | 3½ miles to point C, there and back |
| **Summary**: | A short walk through the fields and woods of a pleasant valley. The picturesque village of Cartmel has a selection of pubs and small shops and an impressive Priory Church to explore |
| **Car parking:** | Signposted off the village square |
| **Disabled toilet:** | Nearest disabled toilet is 2 miles away at Grange-over-Sands (see Walk 6) |
| **Path quality:** | Level but bumpy in places, especially the linear path just beyond point A. Great care needs to be taken on roads |
| **Map:** | Ordnance Survey Explorer OL7 Grid reference: SD377788 |

## Directions

From the car park the walk continues down a broad track away from the village and about 100 yards after crossing the race-track itself, go through a gate to where a track goes off to the left (point A). This left-hand track goes through the woods to the road. Turn left along the road and left again at the first road junction and hence return through the village square and back to the car park. However if you carry straight on at point A the track

**Cartmel Racecourse**

**Cartmel Village Square with the Priory Church in the distance**

soon deteriorates into a very bumpy section for about 200 yards until the next gate is reached. Beyond the gate the track continues through pleasant woodland and it is level and not too bumpy for quite some way. The track then rises up to leave the woods at a gate with a minor road beyond. It is probably advisable to retrace your steps from this point as the road continues steeply uphill.

## Points of interest

The village grew up round an old Priory of Augustinian Monks that was destroyed in 1538 during the dissolution of the Monasteries. The Priory Church was saved because it was also used as the village Church and the gatehouse was similarly reprieved because it was used as the local courthouse. The Priory is an impressive Church, one of the finest in the whole of the country and it is well worth a visit. It has level access throughout. Outside, the Church tower is unusual in that the top of the tower rests diagonally on the lower section. The weathervane, in the

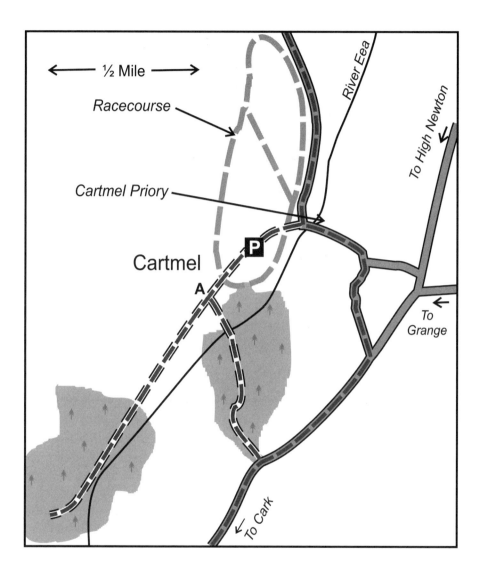

shape of a wolf's head, commemorates the slaying of the last wolf in England at nearby Humphrey Head.

(The racecourse is the smallest National Hunt racecourse in the country and holds its meetings on the spring and summer bank holiday weekends.)

# 6. Grange-over-Sands, Promenade

| | |
|---|---|
| **Distance:** | 2½ miles in total |
| **Summary:** | The promenade provides over a mile of traffic-free level tarmac with stunning views across the Estuary. Grange itself has a good range of small shops though the upper end of Main Street is steep |
| **Car parking:** | Left off Main Street just before the zebra crossing. There are 2 disabled parking spaces. |
| **Disabled toilet:** | On Main Street, just inside the ornamental gardens. RADAR key is required |
| **Path quality:** | Mainly level and all paths surfaced with tarmac |
| **Map:** | Ordnance Survey Explorer OL7 Grid reference: SD409779 |

## Directions

From the car park take the underpass onto the promenade. To the right the promenade continues for about half a mile and passes a small children's playground, whilst turning left takes you past the station to a rocky outcrop. As you reach the station on your return an underpass brings you into the station car park. Turn left in front of the station and continue straight on into the ornamental gardens beyond. The footpath in front of the station has a step so it is necessary to go round this and to mount a two-inch curb near the garden's entrance. On entering the gardens turn immediately right down the path to the lake and follow the path round the side of the lake nearest the road and back to the car park.

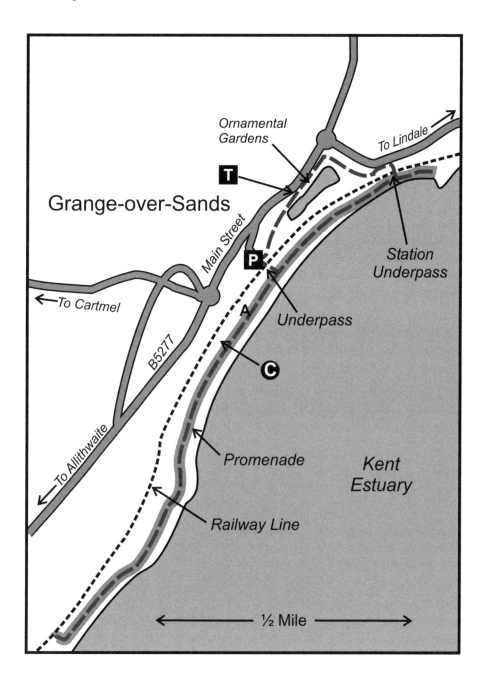

Ornamental Gardens

To Lindale

**T**

Grange-over-Sands

Main Street

Station Underpass

**P**

← To Cartmel

A

Underpass

B5277

**C**

To Allithwaite

Promenade

Kent Estuary

Railway Line

← ½ Mile →

## Points of interest

Grange-over-Sands grew up as a Victorian seaside resort as a result of the building of the railway in 1887. It still retains some of its nineteenth century genteel atmosphere and has a favoured microclimate, being sheltered by the Lake District hills to the North.

Look out for the circular blue (or black) plaques that are located at several points throughout the town, giving information on the various places of interest. For example, near point A, a plaque commemorates the site of a wooden pier where steamers used to bring holidaymakers on day- trips from Morecambe. These excursions took place until 1910 and in 1929 the jetty was swept away in a storm.

As you look out today across the acres of grass on the foreshore its hard to believe how much the estuary must have silted up since then. At weekends in the summer months groups of people are often seen walking across the estuary at low tide from Arnside to Kents Bank, just

**Grange-over-Sands Promenade**

along the coast from Grange. These mud flats are very dangerous and all walks must be led by an experienced local guide. Although they are usually sponsored charity walks today, according to the Monks of Furness Abbey people have been crossing the sands of Morecambe Bay since the middle ages. As you watch groups crossing the sands, even the accompanying tractor and trailer looks minute in the distance and it brings home to you just how large an area this estuary actually is.

A visit to nearby Humphrey Head just 2 or 3 miles away can help to give you some idea of what it must be like out on the mudflats, especially if the tide is low. Take the B5277 towards Allithwaite and just past this village, where the road narrows between two high walls, take the next turn on the left and go past Wraysholme Farm with its old defensive Pele Tower. Go over the level crossing and shortly afterwards turn left and follow the road round until eventually you go over a cattle grid and onto the foreshore where it should be possible to park. If the tide is out and you don't mind getting your wheelchair muddy you might be able to go a short way, for perhaps 50 to 100 yards along the base of the cliff.

The deep channels give some idea of what it must be like for the shrimp and cockle pickers who venture literally miles out from here on old tractors. **If you do decide to try this in your wheelchair stay close to the cliff and take the utmost care as the tide comes in here unbelievably fast**. Traditionally the Morecambe Bay shrimp industry in this area was, and still is, based in Flookborough, the next village along the coast from here. Today the shrimps are raked in by tractor and then they are peeled in Flookborough and potted in Ulverston.

At a height of 172 feet, Humphrey Head has the highest Limestone cliffs in Cumbria and it extends to nearly a mile out onto the mudflats. It is reputedly where John Harrington of Wraysholme killed the last wolf in England in the fifteenth century.

# 7. Broughton-in-Furness

| | |
|---|---|
| **Distance:** | 2 miles there and back |
| **Summary:** | Broughton-in-Furness is an ancient market town with an interesting village square at its centre. The walk follows the track of a disused railway through pleasant countryside |
| **Car parking:** | Park in or near the village square. There is 1 disabled parking space in the square |
| **Disabled toilet:** | About 30 yards from the village square down Knott Lane. RADAR key required |
| **Path quality:** | Gradients are gentle and the path surface is good |
| **Map:** | Ordnance Survey Explorer OL6 Grid reference: SD213876 |

## Directions

The walk starts from the back right-hand corner of the square, down Knott Lane. Follow the lane past the disabled toilet and playing fields on the left and turn left along the disused railway track at the bottom, signposted 'Public Bridleway Woodland 1½ miles'. A narrow path on the left, just after the bridge, leads to a small lake with a convenient seat near the water's edge. Continuing along the path for a short way brings you back to the railway track. After passing over a wooden bridge over a farm track the railway clings to the hillside on a narrow ledge overlooking the valley below. It must have been quite a ride in a rickety old steam train. After this section the track is fenced off and the path continues off to the right, down an embankment, which is too steep for most wheelchairs. Return is by the same route from this point.

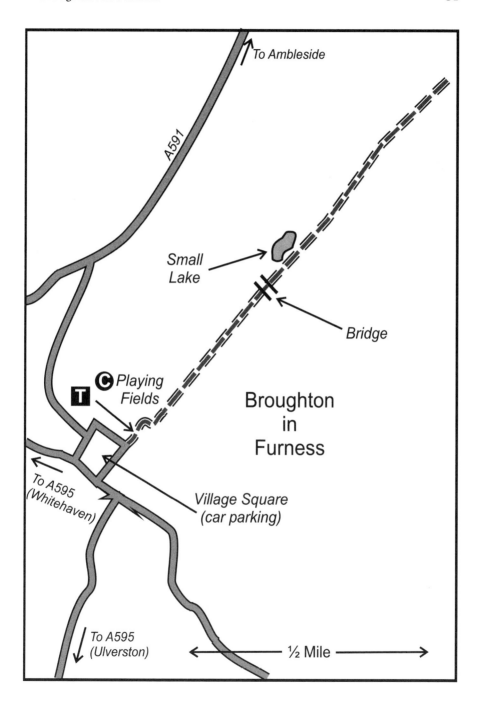

To Ambleside

A591

Small
Lake

Bridge

**C** Playing
**T** Fields

Broughton
in
Furness

To A595
(Whitehaven)

Village Square
(car parking)

To A595
(Ulverston)

½ Mile

**Duddon Ironworks**

# Points of interest

Although there has been a market at Broughton-in-Furness since the sixteenth century the market square itself was rebuilt in 1760 in the Georgian style by the local lord of the manor, John Gilpin Sawrey. The square contains a monument to commemorate the jubilee of King George III in 1810 and also some ancient fish slabs where fish caught locally were sold at market.

The Duddon Ironworks, situated near where the River Duddon crosses under the A595 is well worth a visit. Travelling from Greenodd turn first right immediately after the bridge which is controlled by traffic lights, signposted 'Corney Unsuitable for Caravans'. Duddon Ironworks is about 80 yards down this road on the left, through a gate by a sign 'Duddon Furnace'. There are two gates into the actual ironworks site. The first gate leads to an information board but the rest of the terrain is not suitable for wheelchairs. There is rather better access to the upper part of the site from the second gate however. The Duddon Ironworks is the best example of a charcoal fired blast furnace surviving in Britain today.

It was built in 1736 and produced pig iron up until 1866 that was used to make ships' anchors and chains. It originally had a waterwheel to drive the air bellows and used charcoal from the surrounding woods to smelt the iron ore that was mined locally.

**The railway cutting**

# 8. Torver, Blawith Common

| | |
|---|---|
| **Distance:** | 2 miles there and back |
| **Summary:** | This walk leads directly up a steep farm access road on Blawith Common. The road really is steep in places and is only suitable for fairly powerful wheelchairs and mobility scooters |
| **Car parking:** | Brown Howe Car Park is on the left of the A5084 Torver to Greenodd road, 2 miles South of Torver. There are 3 disabled parking spaces |
| **Disabled toilet:** | On the car park. Baby changing facilities are also available |
| **Path quality:** | Tarmac throughout but **needs care**, as it is very steep in places |
| **Map:** | Ordnance Survey Explorer OL6 Grid reference: SD290911 |

## Directions

From the car park turn left along the road for about 50 yards, taking the first minor lane on the right between the parapets of a small bridge. Continue uphill for about a mile until a gate is reached across the road, beyond which the road is private. Return by the same route. This is a challenging route but it does have dramatic fell-side views, which are in stark contrast to the pastoral charm of the lakeside fields in the valley below.

For those people who do not wish to attempt this walk, Brown Howe Car Park has a pleasant field attached which leads down to the shore of the lake. There are two paths, both of well-compacted shale. The main

**The road on Blawith Common**

**The path down to the lake**

path leads to a seat and then to the water's edge. Alternatively it branches left over a slate bridge and on into the field. The minor path, opposite the toilet block leads to a seat with lovely lakeside views.

## Points of interest

Lake Coniston is 5 miles long and 184 feet deep at its deepest point. The lake was the setting for Arthur Ransome's famous book *Swallows and Amazons*. It is an exciting children's tale about a family of children having adventures sailing on the lake in a small dinghy. Wild Cat Island in the book was based on Peel Island that can be seen from Brown Howe as you look across the lake.

**Peel Island from Brown Howe**

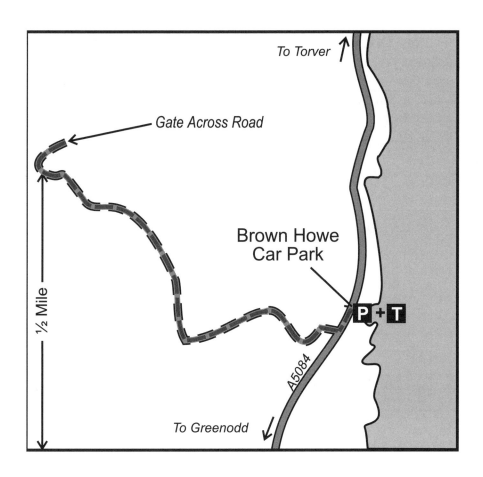

To Torver

Gate Across Road

Brown Howe
Car Park

P + T

½ Mile

A5084

To Greenodd

# 9. Newby Bridge, Fell Foot Park

| | |
|---|---|
| **Distance:** | Circular walk of about ⅓ mile |
| **Summary**: | Eighteen acres of pleasant Victorian gardens, restored by the National Trust, on a steep hillside by the side of Lake Windermere. There is a children's play area |
| **Car parking:** | On the A592 Newby Bridge to Bowness road about one mile from Newby Bridge on the left |
| **Disabled toilet:** | On the main car park and next to the tearoom |
| **Path quality:** | Paths are mostly of fairly loose gravel and rather steep in places |
| **Map**: | Ordnance Survey Explorer OL7 Grid reference: SD382873 |

## Directions

There is a one-way system for cars in the park. Enter at point A and leave at point B. If possible park on the first car park you come to as this has a disabled toilet and there is a tarmac path that leads from here down to the tearoom and shop. At busy times it may be necessary to park in the second car park near point B. However, during the summer season (mid March to end of October) there are staff-driven disabled buggies that will take you and your manual wheelchair down to the tearoom or lakeside. For families, there is a large children's playground, rowing boat hire and a quiz trail and family activity pack is also available.

**The lakeside path**

**Lakeside from Fell Foot Park**

# Points of interest

Across the lake from Fell Foot Park is Lakeside, the terminus for the Windermere Lake Steamers and also for the Lakeside and Haverthwaite Railway which ends right alongside the banking where the steamers tie up. This railway originally went to Barrow-in-Furness but it was closed by British Rail in the 1960's, except for 3½ miles of track, which is still in use today as far as Haverthwaite.

The railway was owned by Henry Schneider, chairman of the largest steelworks in the world in the 1870's, at Barrow-in-Furness. He lived in a large house overlooking Bowness Bay (now The Belsfield Hotel) and each morning he was served breakfast on his own private yacht as travelled down the lake to Lakeside where his own private railway carriage was

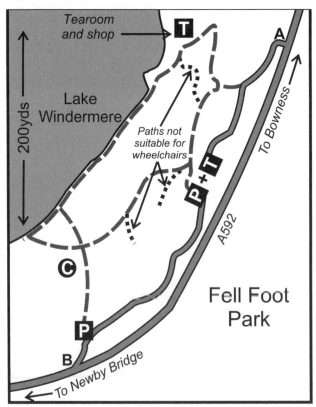

waiting to take him to his works in Barrow-in-Furness.

Schneider's yacht, the Steam Yacht *Esperance*, was built in 1869 from his finest grade of iron. It is now in the Windermere Steamboat Museum and is the oldest boat on the Lloyd's Yacht Register.

# 10. Kendal, Riverside Walk

| | |
|---|---|
| **Distance:** | 2½ miles in total |
| **Summary:** | Although urban in nature this walk along the banks of the River Kent is quite pleasant. There are however some very busy roads to cross, with particular traffic problems at point B (see below) |
| **Car parking:** | Approaching Kendal from the South off the A591, Abbott Hall Museum Car Park is on the right a short way after you enter the one-way system. There are 2 disabled parking spaces |
| **Disabled toilet:** | On the car park and on New Street car park. RADAR key is required |
| **Path quality:** | Mainly level and all paths surfaced with tarmac |
| **Map:** | Ordnance Survey Explorer OL7 Grid reference: SD515923 |

## Directions

From the car park go towards the river to join the riverside path. To the right you pass Kendal Parish Church. The path does continue for some way beyond the bridge but it soon becomes unsurfaced and rather difficult to negotiate in a wheelchair so it's probably advisable to turn back at point A. Going in the other direction you join a minor street just before the bridge at point B. Cross the road here and continue along the side of the road for a short way to a car park. There is no pavement and the road is usually very busy so great care needs to be taken. At the car park, which has another RADAR disabled toilet, the busy roadside can be

**Kendal Parish Church**

avoided by going down the centre of the car park to the far end and onto a footbridge over the river. The path continues along the other bank of the river to point C, where another busy road has to be negotiated. The path reaches a minor street first. Cross here, turn left, cross over the Zebra crossing, turn left, cross the next road and straight on over the bridge. You can now relax as there are no more traffic problems for the rest of the walk. The riverside path continues on the right immediately over the bridge. There is a Pelican crossing at the next road and the path continues for a further half mile until shortly after Dockray Footbridge it turns sharply away from the river and soon deteriorates into an unsurfaced track. Return is by the same route.

## Points of interest

Kendal is an old market town, which grew up in the middle ages as a woollen manufacturing town, hence the town's motto *pannus mihi panis*

**Kendal Riverside Walk**

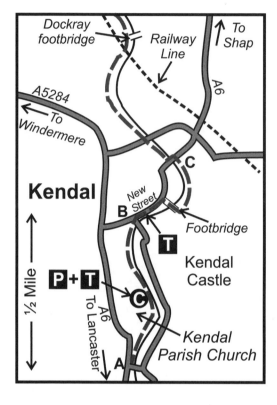

which translates as 'wool is my bread'. It was ideally situated for this industry, being built on the banks of the River Kent.

The main street, running parallel to the river, has narrow yards or alleys, mostly named after their original owners and fortified in the middle ages for protection from Scottish raiders. Many of the yards lead down to the river where the woollen mills were situated.

In the eighteenth century the town became famous for the manufacture of snuff, but today it is probably best know as the home of Kendal mint cake. Marketed as a high-energy food, it found its way on to such high profile expeditions as the exploration of the Antarctic and the conquest of Mount Everest.

Looking across the river from the riverside path the ruins of Kendal Castle, the former home of Katherine Parr, Henry VIII's sixth wife, can be seen on a hill over the rooftops.

Kendal Parish Church is an impressive building, the central aisle of which dates back to the 13th century. There are in fact five aisles today, making it the largest parish Church in Cumbria. It can hold a congregation of 1100 people and is only three feet narrower than York Minster. It has a peel of ten bells the largest of which weighs some 23 cwt (1168 kilos). The 14th century Parr Chapel was built by the Parr family who lived in Kendal Castle and the Church holds copies of prayers that were written by Katherine Parr herself.

# 11. Ravenglass

| | |
|---|---|
| **Distance:** | 2½ miles circular walk |
| **Summary:** | An interesting walk that includes the Ravenglass narrow gauge railway with its turntable and the ruins of a Roman Bath House that is one of the tallest Roman ruins existing in Britain today. The walk continues on a steady climb through woodland and fields to the entrance to Muncaster Castle |
| **Car parking:** | Signposted on approach to village. There are 6 disabled parking spaces |
| **Disabled toilet:** | On left of approach road to car park |
| **Path quality:** | Rather bumpy in places but gradients are not too steep. Involves crossing A595 twice |
| **Map:** | Ordnance Survey Explorer OL6 Grid reference: SD087964 |

## Directions

If you take a stroll down the main street it ends abruptly at the sea with a metal barrier that is used when the tide is high. Returning to the car park, the walk starts in the far corner of the car park on a footbridge across the main line railway. A side path to the left, in front of the children's playground, leads down to the narrow gauge railway station and this is well worth visiting. There is a café on the station, another disabled toilet and across the track there is a small railway museum. To continue on the walk however, return past the children's playground, turn left and after a short way you reach a gate at point A. Turn right up the broad track and after about 200 yards the Roman bath house is on your left. Continuing past the bath house to where the track divides, turn left and after about 200 yards turn left again to climb up through the trees past a small lake on your right. You pass through a gate and the gradient levels out somewhat with fields on either side. After a second gate the octagonal entrance building of Muncaster Castle comes into sight on your right. Turn left about 50 yards before this building and go through the farmyard to the main road. Cross the main road and turn left following the pavement and crossing back over as the pavement changes to the other side of the road. Take the first road to the left back down towards Ravenglass until the gate at point A is reached. Hence return to the car over the railway footbridge.

## Points of interest

The Roman bathhouse is one of the tallest surviving Roman buildings in the UK. It was originally some 88 feet long by 39 feet wide and had a range of warm rooms, like saunas, and a cold plunge.

**The main street in Ravenglass**

**The Roman Bath-House**

Opposite the Roman bath house is the site of the Roman fort *Galannoventa*. The name translates literally as 'the market on the shore' and was part of the sea defences associated with Hadrian's Wall to the North.

Muncaster Castle makes an interesting detour for this walk but a charge is made for admission. It has lovely gardens with many of the paths having fairly good surfaces and gradients. There is also an important owl centre concerned with owl conservation and the ground floor of the castle itself is accessible for wheelchairs.

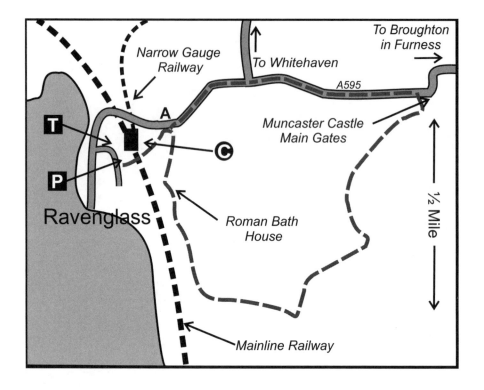

# 12. Eskdale

| | |
|---|---|
| **Distance:** | 1¹/₄ miles circular walk |
| **Summary:** | A pleasant valley stroll on level roads and tracks to see a small 12th Century Church in a delightful riverside setting |
| **Car parking:** | At Dalegarth Station some 2 miles up the valley from Eskdale Green |
| **Disabled toilet:** | On the platform at Dalegarth station, available when the station is open |
| **Path quality:** | Virtually level throughout. The road can get busy with traffic at popular times and the tracks are fairly rough in places |
| **Map:** | Ordnance Survey Explorer OL6 Grid reference: NY173006 |

## Directions

From the station turn left along the road and after about 200 yards turn right down a track signposted 'St. Catherine's Eskdale Parish Church'. This track is not too bad, if you can avoid the potholes, and after about ¹/₂ mile it ends at the river Esk, at the side of the Church. There is a convenient seat to the right in front of the churchyard wall and overlooking the river. The church itself has a step at its entrance, but if you can get inside it has some impressive stained glass windows. Returning back along the track, take the path to the left, just past the Churchyard signposted 'Bridleway only, no motorised vehicles' (point A). This path is something of a challenge to wheelchair users and it can be avoided by returning to the road of course.

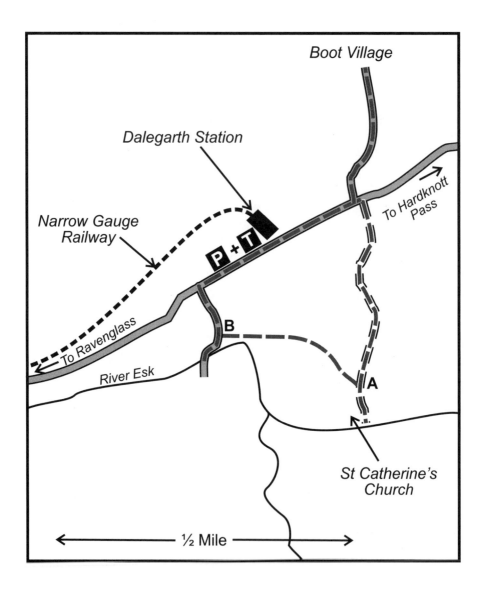

**St Catherine's Church**

# Points of interest

The narrow gauge railway was built in 1875 to carry iron ore from Eskdale down to the main line railway at Ravenglass. It was taken over by the Preservation Society in 1960. The railway line is seven miles long, and has the oldest working 15-inch gauge locomotive in the world, the engine *River Irt,* which was built in 1894. The railway is known by the locals as 'La'al Ratty' which is local dialect for 'little narrow way' and this has lead to the creation of a children's water-vole stationmaster character of the same name.

There are disabled toilets at the Stations at Ravenglass and Eskdale and the train is accessible for wheelchairs.

# 13. Grizedale Forest

**Distance:** Riddings Trail: 1¼ miles from car park and back. Millwood trail: ¾ mile linear path from visitor centre to point B and back

**Summary:** The Grizedale Visitor Centre is set in a beautiful valley in the heart of the extensive Grizedale Forest. It has a full range of facilities, which at the time of writing are undergoing major redevelopment, funded partly by the European Regional Development Fund. Visitors' facilities have been temporarily relocated but they are all well signposted

**Car parking:** Approaching from Hawkshead the car park is about 300 yards past the visitor centre on the left. As you enter the car park turn left and there are 3 disabled parking spaces (plus 2 spaces for disabled mini buses) on the left at the top of the hill

**Disabled toilet:** At the visitor centre

**Path quality:** Riddings Trail: tarmac surface and fairly gentle slopes. Millwood Trail: good surface and level

**Map:** Ordnance Survey Explorer OL6 Grid reference: SD335943

**The Grizedale valley from the Riddings Trail**

# Directions

### The Riddings Trail

This footpath, in the grounds of the now demolished Grizedale Hall, has been developed specially for wheelchairs and pushchairs and has a tarmac surface throughout. The path starts from in front of the Yan Building, which is signposted from the car park. There are sculptures to be seen every few yards along the way, many of them of interest to young children. The short un-surfaced linear path from point A should not be missed because it leads to a clearing in the trees with a superb view over the Grizedale valley.

### The Millwood Trail

From the Car park follow signs for the visitor centre and then for the 'Go Ape' attraction. The path starts from near the large wooden woodcutter

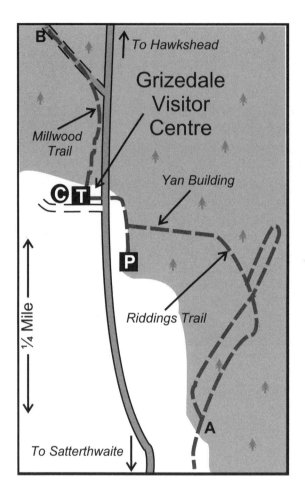

sculpture near the Go Ape cabin. Only the section from the visitor centre to point B, where the path leaves the tarmac roadway, is suitable for wheelchairs as there are steps beyond here. This walk should not be missed because of the Go Ape attraction which is a spectacular network of aerial walkways high up in large pine trees.

## Points of interest

Grizedale Forest extends to some 8,000 acres and is the home to both roe and red deer. It was acquired by the Forestry Commission in 1937 and was the first of their forests to cater for visitors.

The now demolished Grizedale Hall, which was sited at the top of the car park near the new Yan building, was used in the Second World War as a prisoner of war camp. In particular it gained fame for the attempted escape of Oberleutenant Franz Von Werra in 1940 whose story is featured in the 1957 film *The One Who Got Away*.

**Sculpture near start of Millwood Trail**

# 14. Hawkshead

| | |
|---|---|
| **Distance:** | ½ mile circular walk |
| **Summary:** | This short walk of less than half a mile enables you to escape the Hawkshead tourist trap for a short while and get a glimpse of the beautiful surrounding countryside |
| **Car parking:** | In the village, signposted. There are 4 disabled parking spaces on the right of the road and 7 spaces on the left |
| **Disabled toilet:** | Toilet block on the car park. RADAR key required |
| **Path quality:** | Gradients are not too steep, except for a very steep path up to the Church. Path surfaces are good |
| **Map:** | Ordnance Survey Explorer OL7 Grid reference: SD353981 |

## Directions

From the car park in the village go up the road past the toilet block and straight on through the gates to the old grammar school. Continue past the school up a steep tarmac drive into the Churchyard. This is probably one of the hilliest Churchyards in the country and it's well worth pausing to take in the views over the village. The path continues straight ahead and out of the Churchyard by a stone slab wall. The path levels out and is now of finely crushed stone which is excellent for wheelchairs. At the next gate take the broader right-hand path signposted 'Walker Ground'. Continue to a T-junction and turn right to the village down a tarmac lane.

As you enter the village the first or second street to the right brings you back to the car park.

## Points of interest

Hawkshead's main claim to fame seems to be the fact that William Wordsworth went to school here in the 1780s and his school desk is on view in the old grammar school complete with his name carved on it! The walk also passes Ann Tyson's cottage where Wordsworth lodged when he was at school. Beatrix Potter, whose house, Hill Top is at nearby Near Sawrey, also used to own several properties in the town that she later gave to the National Trust. Some of her original work is exhibited in one of them, The Beatrix Potter Gallery.

Despite the many tourist shops the fact that cars are banned from the centre of the village means that it is easy to wander round these quaint

**St Michael and All Angels' Church from the path**

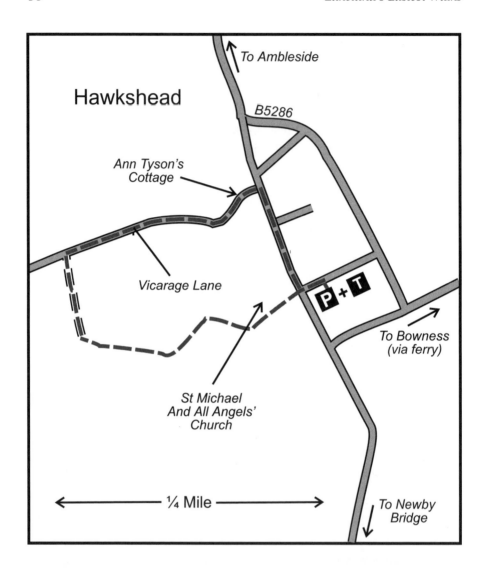

To Ambleside

Hawkshead

B5286

Ann Tyson's
Cottage

Vicarage Lane

P + T

To Bowness
(via ferry)

St Michael
And All Angels'
Church

←——— ¼ Mile ———→

To Newby
Bridge

streets and imagine what it must have been like in Wordsworth's time. Regardless of the William Wordsworth or Beatrix Potter connection Hawkshead village is worth a visit in its own right, preferably outside the tourist season when it is less crowded.

**A quiet corner of Hawkshead**

# 15. Far Sawrey, Windermere Lake

| | |
|---|---|
| **Distance:** | 1½ miles there and back |
| **Summary:** | A pleasant lakeside walk on a quiet access road through peaceful unfenced parkland |
| **Car parking:** | Coming from Hawkshead the road eventually descends to the shore of Lake Windermere, over a stone wall, and you turn left along here where a large 'keep clear' sign is painted on the road (by a sign saying '8T weight limit on ferry'). Harrowslack car park is on the left of this road, just after a cattle grid |
| **Disabled toilet:** | The toilet block near to the ferry has disabled toilets in both the Gents and the Ladies |
| **Path quality:** | Tarmac road with gentle gradients |
| **Map:** | Ordnance Survey Explorer OL7 Grid reference: SD388957 |

## Directions

From the car park the route is simply to continue along this quiet tarmac road for about ¾ mile until it ends at a cattle grid and gate across the road. Return by the same route. The road passes through open fields with fine views across the lake.

## Points of interest

Hill Top Farm, Beatrix Potter's home where she wrote many of her books is situated at Near Sawrey, just 2 miles up the road from the ferry towards Hawkshead. After her marriage in 1913 she moved to nearby

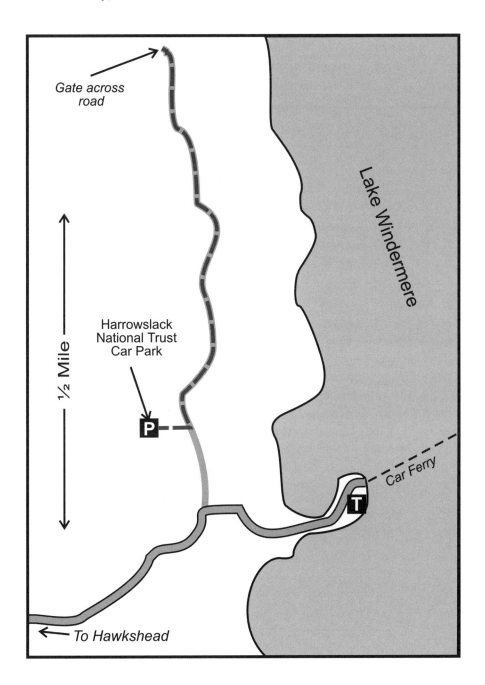

Gate across
road

Lake Windermere

½ Mile

Harrowslack
National Trust
Car Park

**P**

Car Ferry

**T**

← To Hawkshead

**The lakeside road**

Castle Cottage but returned to Hill Top to write her books. When she died in 1943 she left Hill Top to the National Trust on the understanding that it remained furnished exactly as she had left it. It is a very popular tourist visit, but only the ground floor is accessible for wheelchairs. If you do intend to go in a wheelchair it is necessary to telephone them beforehand. (Tel: 015394 36269).

**The ferry from this walk**

The Windermere car ferry was built in 1990 and can carry up to 18 cars and over 100 passengers. It is pulled from one side of the lake to the other by a chain and boats must be careful to pass behind the ferry, not in front of it, because the chain under tension is very near the surface of the lake.

# 16. Windermere Lake, Red Nab

| | |
|---|---|
| **Distance:** | 2 miles there and back |
| **Summary**: | A pleasant traffic free lakeside woodland walk – a walk for all seasons. In the winter the leaves do not hide the views across the lake, whilst in the summer these same leaves provide much welcome shade |
| **Car parking:** | At the end of the lane from High Wray |
| **Disabled toilet:** | Nearest one at Hawkshead 3 miles away |
| **Path quality:** | Good surface and level throughout |
| **Map**: | Ordnance Survey Explorer OL7 Grid reference: SD386995 |

## Directions
Approaching High Wray from Hawkshead, turn right at the grass triangle signposted 'Ferry 3 unfit for vehicles after I mile'. The car park is by the lake as the tarmac ends. From the car park the path leads north along the lakeshore for about a mile. There is a bench overlooking the lake after the first gate and there really is not much point proceeding any further. If you do continue on, a second gate is soon reached and after this the path becomes steep and very bumpy.

## Points of interest
Claife Woods are delightful, but a local legend has it that they are haunted by the 'Claife Crier', the ghost of a Furness Abbey monk, who's aim in life was to rescue fallen women. He was rejected in love, went mad

and after his death his spirit lived on in Claife Woods. The story is that on a wild and stormy night long ago, the ferryman heard a cry from the opposite bank, so he rowed across to pick up his fare. The terrified man returned alone unable to speak and died shortly afterwards of a fever. After that no ferryman would work after dark and it was said that on stormy nights eerie cries were often heard coming from the opposite bank. Eventually the ghost was exorcised and the spirit confined to a quarry in the woods. Even today some local people will not go into Claife Woods at night!

**The lakeside path near Red Nab**

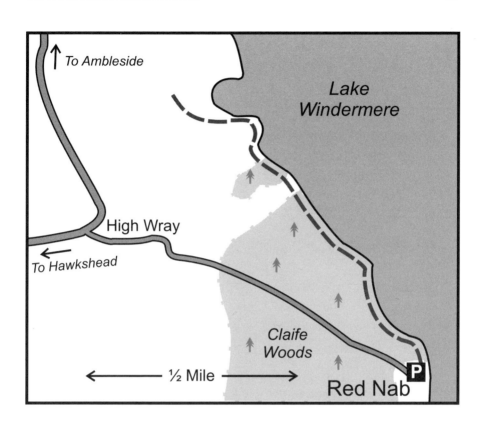

# 17. Bowness-on-Windermere, Cockshott Point

| | |
|---|---|
| **Distance:** | 1½ miles circular walk |
| **Summary:** | On a nice day, out of season, Bowness makes a delightful visit but at other times Bowness does get very busy and it can be a nightmare in a wheelchair! |
| **Car parking:** | On Glebe Road. There are 3 disabled parking spaces |
| **Disabled toilet:** | Near the tourist information office at point A and on Ferry Nab Car Park. Both toilets require a RADAR key |
| **Path quality:** | Very good and fairly level |
| **Map:** | Ordnance Survey Explorer OL7 Grid reference: SD399967 |

## Directions

The car park is situated about 300 yards along Glebe Road which runs along the waterfront at Bowness. Turn left along Glebe Road from the front of the car park and where the road bends sharply left round the car park, carry straight on, on a footpath through the trees to a wheelchair adapted kissing gate. The path continues through a field round Cockshott Point with excellent views over the lake. At the next kissing gate turn right if you want to see the car ferry at close quarters, otherwise turn left and follow the path across a field and back onto Glebe Road. Cross the road and take the lane opposite, with a miniature golf course on one side and the cemetery on the other. The lane leads

**Belle Island from Cockshott Point**

back to the A592 at point A. If you can manage a steep gradient take the path to the left along the side of the miniature golf course and hence back to the car park. Otherwise go forward to the main road and turn left down Glebe Road, past the tourist information centre and back to the car.

## Points of interest

At over ¹/₂ mile in length Belle Island is the largest of Lake Windermere's 18 islands and the only one ever to be inhabited. The governor of the Roman fort at the head of the lake at Waterhead had a villa here, and more recently the island was sold to Isabella Curwen after the English Civil War and named after her. Her descendants lived on the island until 1993. Bowness developed as a tourist hotspot as a result of the arrival of the railway to nearby Windermere in 1847. Nothing much has changed, as likewise today it's the first port of call for numerous visitors who arrive from the south. On a nice day, out of season, Bowness makes a delightful visit but at other times Bowness does get very busy and it can be a nightmare in a wheelchair!

St Martin's Church, just up the hill from Bowness Bay is an interesting Church with impressive stained glass, murals and ancient artefacts including an octagonal sandstone font dating from the 13th century.

**Boats in Bowness Bay with St Martin's Church Tower on the sky-line**

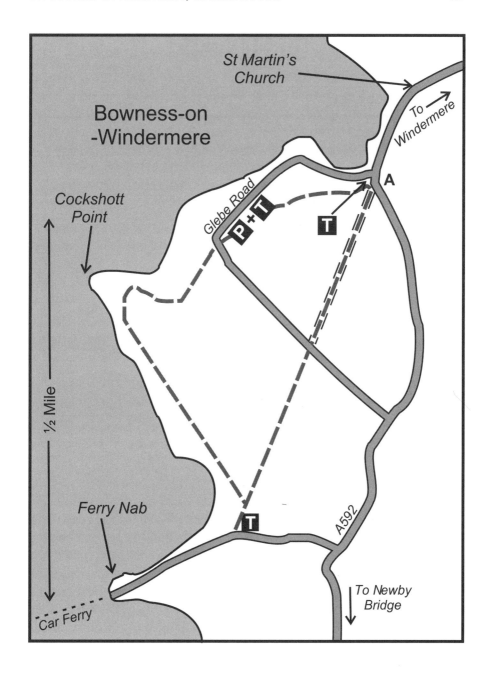

# 18. Staveley

| | |
|---|---|
| **Distance:** | 4½ miles there and back |
| **Summary:** | A linear walk on a very quiet farm access road along the Kent Valley with a final climb up the valley side to gain long distance views over the surrounding countryside |
| **Car parking:** | Lay-by on the right of the road to Kentmere on the outskirts of Staveley |
| **Disabled toilet:** | New Road car park, Kendal, 4¾ mile away. (see Walk 10) |
| **Path quality:** | Tarmac with gentle gradients up to point A and then steep uphill. The road from Staveley to Scroggs Bridge can be busy with traffic |
| **Map:** | Ordnance Survey Explorer OL7 Grid reference: SD470988 |

## Directions

From the lay-by continue down the road until it crosses the river at Scroggs Bridge. Take the minor road straight on at this point, signposted 'Browfoot Lane No Through Road'. After about 1½ miles the road turns sharply left and continues steeply uphill for another ½ mile before ending at a T-junction with a rough track that I found to be too rough for my wheelchair. There is a good view over the surrounding countryside from up here and on the return journey my powered wheelchair speeded up on the downhill section so much that it reminded me of freewheeling down similar hills in my cycling days. Whilst this was great fun, an appropriate amount of care must be taken when negotiating this decent.

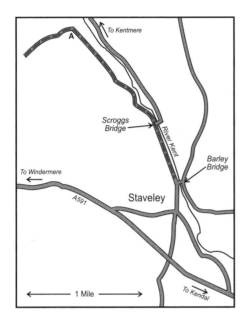

**The Kent Valley from the road**

# 19. Windermere, Lake District Visitor Centre, Brockhole

**Distance:** Depending on the route taken you would probably do well in excess of ½ mile exploring the grounds

**Summary:** The visitor centre, run by the National Park Authority, gives an excellent introduction to the Lake District, and the extensive grounds are a delight to explore. There is a large children's adventure playground

**Car parking:** On the left of the A591 Windermere to Ambleside road. There is a small disabled car park next to the Visitors' Centre accessed through the main car park. Alternatively, when the centre is open, a staff driven electric buggy is available to take you from the main car park up to the house

**Disabled toilet:** On the main car park and in the visitor centre

**Path quality:** The path down from the house is steep (see below) but paths below the terraced gardens are fairy level with good surfaces

**Map:** Ordnance Survey Explorer OL7 Grid reference: SD470988

**Brockhole Visitor Centre**

# Directions

The Grounds are open daily throughout the year and the visitor centre is open from mid-February to the end of October. A detailed map of the grounds showing wheelchair routes is available from the visitor centre. There are also manual wheelchairs for use inside the visitor centre and electric wheelchairs for use in the gardens, available free of charge.

The 30 acres of gardens are an absolute delight in their setting besides the lake. The formal terraced gardens near the house have steep slopes however and some of them also have steps. Probably the best way down to the lake, where there is a lakeside walk through the trees, is to take the path, which starts just behind the toilet block on the main car park. The lakeside walk does however become unsuitable for wheelchairs as it turns inland away from the lake, so it is necessary to return by the same route.

The house itself contains displays and exhibitions about the Lake District National Park. There is also a gift shop and a café/restaurant with spectacular views over the gardens and the lake.

## Points of interest

Brockhole was originally a private residence built in 1898 by William Gaddum who was a silk merchant from Manchester. Beatrix Potter was a visitor to Brockhole in its early days as Mrs. Gaddum was her cousin.

The gardens were laid out by the landscape gardener Thomas Mawson who designed the grounds specifically to enhance the dramatic views from the house of the lake and the fells beyond.

Today the National Park Authority have produced interesting displays about the Lake District in the house and they arrange a series of events throughout the season to help visitors learn more about a variety of Lake District topics.

**The lakeside walk**

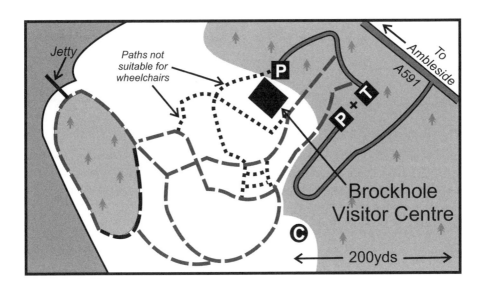

# 20. Windermere, Holehird Gardens

| | |
|---|---|
| **Distance:** | About ½ mile in total depending on the route chosen |
| **Summary:** | The Lakeland Horticultural Society runs this garden which is a must for garden lovers. There are impressive long distance views over Lake Windermere |
| **Car parking:** | The Gardens are on the right of the A592 about a mile from Windermere, signposted 'Holehird Gardens'. There is one disabled parking space on the main car park and two more near the disabled toilet |
| **Disabled toilet:** | By the offices at the side of the walled garden |
| **Path quality:** | The walled garden is level and paved. There is a moderate slope down the road to the lower terrace, which is also level |
| **Map:** | Ordnance Survey Explorer OL7 Grid reference: NY414010 |

## Directions

The path between point A and point B is of loose pebbles and grass. I have included it because there is a wooden bench at point B with a spectacular view over part of Lake Windermere to the fells beyond.

There are several other paths in the garden that are not shown on the map because they are not really suitable for wheelchair users. In particular paths in the upper garden have loose pebbles, they are steep

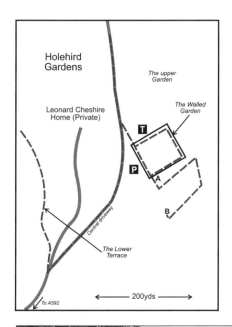

**View from the central driveway**

in places and some of them have steps. There are also steps at the end of the lower terrace so it is necessary to retrace your steps from here.

## Points of interest

These gardens were developed from an abandoned rock garden belonging to Holehird Mansion in the 1970's. The ten-acre site is run entirely by volunteers who are all members of the Lakeland Horticultural Society. Admission is free but donations are welcome. The gardens include the National Plant Collections for Astilbe, Hydrangea and Polystichum and information on these and other horticultural topics are available on site from their specialist library. We have also picked up several useful tips by chatting to the volunteers themselves.

**The Walled Garden**

# 21. Coniston

| | |
|---|---|
| **Distance:** | 4 miles there and back including branch paths |
| **Summary:** | This is a very pleasant walk that follows the side of the road for much of the way but you would hardly know it as the path is separated from the road by a high hedge. There are two short linear branch routes that are well worth taking. Coniston is an interesting village, with its connections to John Ruskin and Donald Campbell and there are spectacular views across the lake on several parts of this walk |
| **Car parking:** | At the end of the lake at Monk Coniston where there are 3 disabled parking spaces. Also in Coniston at the Tilberthwaite Road Car Park there are 3 disabled parking spaces and at Coniston Boating Centre (point D) there are 2 disabled parking spaces next to the disabled toilet and a further 5 spaces overlooking the lake next to the Bluebird Café |
| **Disabled toilet:** | Next to the car park at Monk Coniston. Also on Tilberthwaite Road Car Park where a RADAR key is required and also at Coniston Boating Centre |
| **Path quality:** | Virtually level throughout with a good surface except for about 100 yards. of shoreline on the branch path between point C and point D. This is very bumpy and has loose pebbles in places |
| **Map:** | Ordnance Survey Explorer OL7 Grid reference: SD317978 |

# Directions

Take the B5285 from Conistion to Hawkshead and just after passing the
end of the lake turn right down the minor road towards Brantwood. The
car park is on the right just past the lake.

From the car park at Monk Coniston there is a short lakeside walk
past the toilet block and down to the jetty from which small launches ply
up and down the lake. The view from here looks across the lake to
Coniston and the fells beyond.

**View down length of lake from Monk Coniston**

Returning to the car park follow the road left past the end of the lake
using the path on the right hand side of the road. At the T-junction cross
over the road to the path behind the hedge (point A). If you turn right
the path continues for about ¼ mile, mostly behind the hedge, until the
minor road is reached at point B. The footpath continues to Tarn Hows
but it is not suitable for wheelchairs. Returning to point A and
continuing straight on towards Coniston there are spectacular fell-side
views to the right. About 100 yards after the Waterhead Hotel there is a

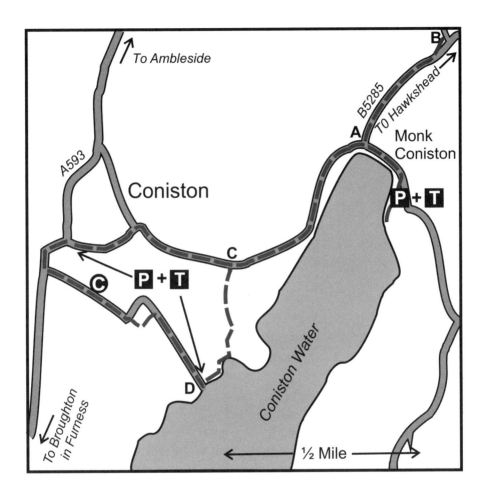

way-mark post in a gap in the roadside hedge (point C). Cross the road and go through the gate at the side of the cattle grid, signposted 'Permitted Footpath Coniston Boating Centre'. Continue down the tarmac access road until just before the house at the end and take a short path on the right across the field, over a bridge and onto the shore of the lake. Turn right and continue to the boating centre and the jetty (point D). The path is rather rough along this short section. From the jetty follow the road into the village. From the Boating Centre there is a fine footpath alongside the road and the stream. If you follow this and

**The roadside path**

then cross over the stream by the footbridge and go through the Lakeside Workshops to rejoin the road it avoids a narrow road-bridge. You can then continue along the pavement up to the main road where you turn right and go over the footbridge at the side of the main bridge in Coniston. There is no footpath for about 50 yards around the Church so great care is needed. Continuing down the main road brings you out of the village and where the road narrows somewhat to go over a bridge. There is no footpath for about 100 yards and great care also needs to be taken on this section. It is probably advisable to cross the road at a dropped kerb about 50 yards before the bridge and continue over the bridge on the left side of the road. The path behind the hedge then starts just over the bridge and this brings you back to point C from where you can retrace your steps to the car.

Note: If you are at all worried about negotiating the lakeshore it might be a better idea to continue straight on at point C and go directly into

Coniston. If you do this and wish to go down to Coniston Boating Centre, continue past the Church and take the first left, signposted 'Lake Road leading to Beck Yeat'.

## Points of interest

The Ruskin Museum in the centre of Coniston was set up as a tribute to John Ruskin In 1901, shortly after his death. Since then it has been expanded to include information and artefacts from the whole area around Coniston including a section about Donald Campbell's water speed exploits. Ruskin was an important Victorian writer and philosopher who lived for the last 27 years of his life at Brantwood, the large house in the trees seen across the lake from the jetty at Coniston. Although a relatively old building the Brantwood Trust has made efforts to make the house accessible, at least on the ground floor when the major part of the museum is situated. There is also a disabled toilet and limited access to the gardens. An admission fee is charged.

Coniston Water shot to fame nationally in the 1960's as the venue for Donald Campbell's attempts at the water speed record. He was killed here in 1967 trying to break the 300 mph barrier. His grave can be seen in St. Andrew's Churchyard in the centre of Coniston. John Ruskin is buried here also, his grave being marked by a large Celtic cross.

The steamboat Gondola makes an impressive sight in summer months with its plume of white smoke as it carries passengers the length of the lake. It was originally built in 1859 and restored by The National Trust in 1980. Unfortunately it cannot take passengers in wheelchairs.

# 22. Coniston, Tarn Hows

| | |
|---|---|
| **Distance:** | The linear walk, from the disabled car park, is about ½ mile there and back. The circular walk round the Tarn, best accessed from the main car park, is about 1¾ miles in length |
| **Summary:** | Tarn Hows, one of the most picturesque and most popular tarns in the Lake District, is in fact a shallow man-made lake, created in the nineteenth century by building a dam across a stream which drained an area of marshland. It was made specifically as a tourist attraction |
| **Car parking:** | The disabled car park has 4 parking spaces |
| **Disabled toilet:** | At the back of the main car park. RADAR key is required |
| **Path quality:** | The linear path has a fairly good surface of loose pebbles with gentle to moderate inclines. The path from the road down to the Tarn is fairly steep and pebbly. The path round the Tarn is fairly level and smooth but with one or two short steep sections |
| **Map:** | Ordnance Survey Explorer OL7 Grid reference: SD328993 |

## Directions

Tarn Hows is signposted from the B5285 Coniston to Hawkshead road. As you approach Tarn Hows there is a small disabled car park on the right. Leading from the car park is a level linear track, which has lovely

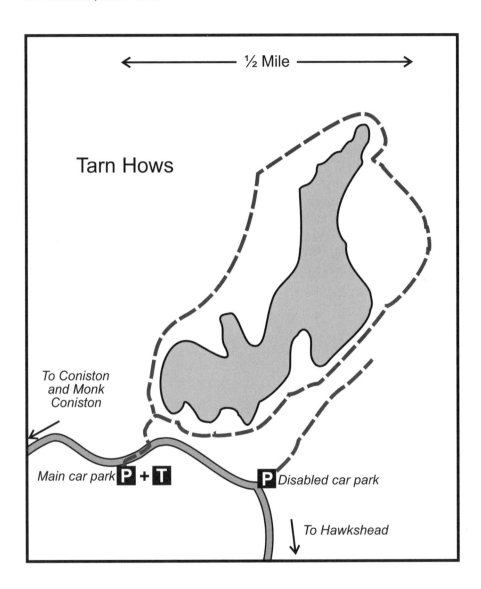

views over the tarn. After about ¼ mile the track divides and becomes too rough for wheelchairs. For the path around the tarn it is preferable to park in the main car park. The path is signposted 'To The Tarn' and is about 100 yards back up the road. Turn left off the road taking the path down to the tarn to join a path which leads all the way round the tarn.

# Points of interest

There is a small information centre next to the toilets in the main car park with displays relating to how the tarn has been developed, the Monk Coniston estate and Beatrix Potter's legacy. Briefly, Tarn Hows originally consisted of three smaller tarns, which were formed into a single body of water in the 1860s by means of a small dam. The tarn was landscaped about the same time by the planting trees. By 1900 it was an important beauty spot and tourist attraction. The land surrounding Tarn Hows was bought by Beatrix Potter in 1930. She sold half the land, including the tarn, to the National Trust and left the other half to them in her will.

**The linear track**

**Tarn Hows from the linear track**

At popular times, when the National Trust warden has his Landrover on site, children's 'Tracker Packs' are available from him, giving details of what to look out for on the walk.

After leaving the car park it's worth turning left and continuing down this road to meet the B5285. There are spectacular views across towards the Coniston Fells on your right as you descend.

# 23. Seascale

| | |
|---|---|
| **Distance:** | 2½ miles in total |
| **Summary:** | This walk follows a lovely coastal path from the small seaside village of Seascale. There is a very nice sandy beach and there are long distance views to St Bees head to the North |
| **Car parking:** | At the beach. There are 4 disabled parking spaces |
| **Disabled toilet:** | On the car park. RADAR key is required |
| **Path quality:** | Gradients are mainly gentle and the surfaces vary from tarmac to rather bumpy but overall they are fairly good |
| **Map:** | Ordnance Survey Explorer OL6 Grid reference: NY036009 |

## Directions

The coastal path passes in front of the car park. If you take it to the South it leads right onto the beach. From the car park you first of all pass a grassy area and then take the lower path on top of the sea wall. The beach here is rocky but soon gives way to sand. This path continues for a couple of hundred yards or so and then ends in a short ramp onto the sand itself.

The main part of this walk however is along the cliff path to the North. The easiest way to get onto this path is to go to the corner of the car park near the railway bridge and take the road to the left signposted 'National Cycle Route 72, Sellafield 1¾, Whitehaven 16'. This road goes

**The cliff-top path**

up behind the toilets on the left and the railway station on the right. Continue forward to join a path which leads northwards along the top of low sandy cliffs with superb sea views. After about $^3/_4$ mile the Sellafield Nuclear Site comes into view and at point B the path turns inland by the side of a small river inlet and under a railway bridge. The path does continue for another half mile to Sellafield railway station but it passes between high security fences with the only views being of heavy industrial sprawl. Unless you want to see Sellafield at close quarters it is advisable to turn back at this point to return to Seascale.

# Points of interest
Seascale developed as a seaside resort in the latter half of the nineteenth century with the building of the railway but declined somewhat in the latter half of the twentieth century with the building of three nuclear

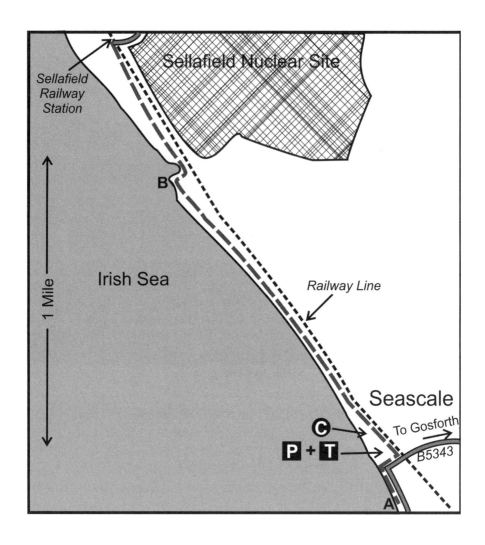

reactors right on its doorstep.    If you do decide to continue your walk
beyond point B the background information which follows might be of
some interest.

In total the Sellafield Nuclear Site employs some 10,000 people
contributing massively to the local economy. The Windscale reactor
produced the country's first weapons grade plutonium in the 1950s

whilst the Calder Hall reactor, built in 1956, was the World's first commercial nuclear power station. The Sellafield reactor reprocesses spent fuel from reactors around the world into reusable fuel and highly radioactive by-products, which need to be stored for thousands of years.

The nuclear site has not been free from incident or controversy over the years with at least twenty serious incidents involving a discharge of radioactive material. In 1957 the Windscale reactor caught fire, resulting in the contamination of local livestock and the destruction of produce from local farms. Also in the early days dilute radioactive material was actually dumped by pipeline into the sea with the result that today the Irish Sea is one of the most contaminated seas in the World. It became so serious that the local beach had to be closed for a time in 1983. In the 1990s studies found that the local population showed a higher than normal number of people suffering from leukaemia. In 2005 a leakage of radioactive material was not discovered for nine months. Fortunately it was inside the plant and did not escape into the environment.

**The Sellafield Nuclear Site from Point B**

# 24. Ambleside, Rothay Park

| | |
|---|---|
| **Distance:** | Circular walk 1 mile. Linear walk 2½ miles there and back |
| **Summary:** | Rothay Park provides wide-open spaces right next to the busy streets of Ambleside as the photograph opposite shows. The quiet road over the footbridge beyond the park makes an excellent extension to the walk |
| **Car parking:** | On the left of the A591 just out of Ambleside town centre travelling towards Grasmere. There are 8 disabled parking spaces |
| **Disabled toilet:** | On the car park. RADAR key is required |
| **Path quality:** | Level, good surfaces mostly of tarmac. The footbridge over the River Rothay is steep |
| **Map:** | Ordnance Survey Explorer OL7 Grid reference: NY377046 |

## Directions

From the car park turn left along Rydal Road past the Fire Station and Police Station, then first left again down Stoney Lane. At the end of this short lane take the path on the right through a gate. This gate leads down to a picturesque but steep footbridge over the River Rothay. The road beyond is very quiet and makes a nice linear walk in either direction but my recommendation would be to turn to the right and hence away from the town. It is possible to continue along here for about 1¼ miles before the A591 is reached. Returning to the footbridge a path to the

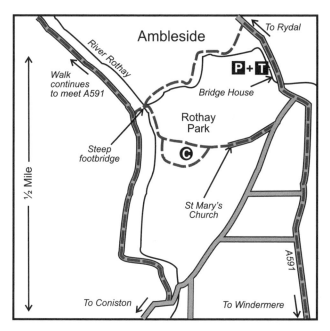

**St Mary's Church from Rothay Park**

**Bridge House**

right immediately over the bridge brings you into Rothay Park with a variety of level tarmac paths to explore. If you then head towards the spire of St Mary's Church a gateway brings you into Vicarage Lane which leads to Compston Road and up into Ambleside itself. Turning left at the traffic lights at the top of Compston Road, it's just a short walk back to the car park past the aptly named and unmistakeable Bridge House.

## Points of interest

Bridge House was built in the eighteenth century on a bridge to avoid paying land tax. It was originally an apple store for Ambleside Hall and is reputed to once have been the home of a family of eight! It is now owned by The National Trust and must surely be one of their more unusual information centres.

St Mary's Church, designed by Sir George Gilbert Scott in the 1850s is one of the few Lake District Churches to have a spire. There is a large mural inside showing the Ambleside rush-bearing ceremony. This takes place on the first Saturday in July and dates back to a time when rushes were used to cover the floor of the church. The rushes were changed annually on this date and nowadays the ceremony involves a procession through the town to take rushes and flowers to the Church.

# 25. Little Langdale, Blea Tarn

| | |
|---|---|
| **Distance:** | ½ mile there and back |
| **Summary:** | This short walk is probably as near to mountaineering as it is possible to get from a wheelchair! It's a long way to come for such a short walk but the dramatic mountain scenery is superb |
| **Car parking:** | Opposite the Tarn at the top of the pass between Great Langdale and Little Langdale |
| **Disabled toilet:** | The nearest one is 9 miles away at Ambleside (see Walk 24) |
| **Path quality:** | A fairly good pebbly surface with gentle to moderate gradients |
| **Map:** | Ordnance Survey Explorer OL6 Grid reference: NY296043 |

## Directions

From Ambleside, take the sign for Coniston and after a couple of miles take the right fork at Skelwith Bridge, signposted 'Elterwater, Langdale'. Continue down this road past Elterwater and Chapel Style and at the head of Great Langdale, opposite The Old Dungeons Ghyll Hotel, the road turns sharply left to take you up a steep mountain pass. The Tarn is situated about a mile from the top of the pass, with the car park opposite. From the car park, cross the road and go through the gate opposite. Follow the path down to the footbridge over the stream and bear right to follow the path through the trees to a stile at the far end of the Tarn. Return is by the same route. There is a short path leading onto a promontory overlooking the Tarn with spectacular views of the Langdale Pikes.

## Points of interest

The Langdale Pikes are at their most impressive when viewed from the South as their crags fall some 2000 feet to the Langdale Valley below. There are three main peaks that together form a distinctive skyline that can be recognised from many distant vantage points. The peaks are Harrison Stickle (2,415 ft.), Pike of Stickle (2,326 ft.) and Loft Crag (2,238 ft.). A 'stickle' is a hill with a steep rocky top and a 'pike' is a hill with a peak.

**The Langdale Pikes from the path**

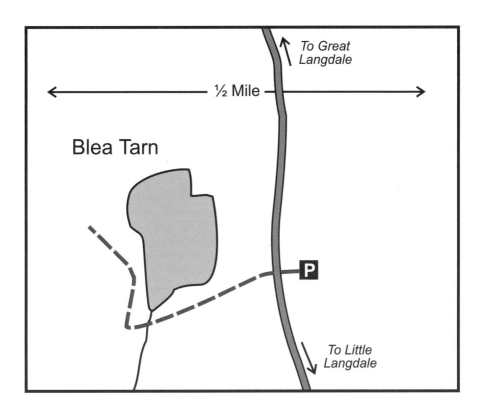

To Great
Langdale

½ Mile

Blea Tarn

P

To Little
Langdale

# 26. Grasmere

| | |
|---|---|
| **Distance:** | 1 mile circular walk and ¾ mile linear path there and back |
| **Summary:** | A riverside walk on a wheelchair friendly footpath and a pleasant tourist village with the strongest of connections to William Wordsworth |
| **Car parking:** | Broadgate car park. There are 5 disabled parking spaces |
| **Disabled toilet:** | The disabled toilet is situated on College Street, next to the Methodist Church. RADAR key required |
| **Path quality:** | Level tarmac throughout |
| **Map:** | Ordnance Survey Explorer OL7 Grid reference: NY338077 |

## Directions

Coming from Ambleside, go straight on at the roundabout and take the next turning on the left opposite the Swan Hotel signposted 'Grasmere Village'. Broadgate car park is about ¼ mile down here on the left. The walk starts from the car park by crossing the river on a bridge near the disabled parking spaces. Follow it round to the Churchyard, where Wordsworth's grave can be seen. You can explore the village from here and then return either by the same path or out along Broadgate itself and back to the car park that way. Dove Cottage, the former home of William Wordsworth, can be seen by taking the road out of the village which passes the front gate of the Church, go over the bridge and after about ¼ mile cross the A591. Turn right and Dove Cottage is situated a short way up the lane to the left. Wheelchair access to the cottage is limited to the ground floor.

## Points of interest

Grasmere is dominated by the tourist trade which is centred round its association with William Wordsworth. He was an important poet who helped establish the romantic movement in England at the end of the eighteenth century. He lived in the area from 1799 when he moved into Dove Cottage with his sister Dorothy. In 1803 he married Mary Hutchinson whom he had known since childhood and his first child John was born the following year. Dorothy continued to live with the family and got on well with Mary. In 1808 the Wordsworths moved to a larger house in the Grasmere area, then to a house near St. Oswald's Church and finally in 1813 they settled at Rydal Mount, which is situated up a lane just past the far end of Rydal Water. William Wordsworth died in 1850 at the age of 80 and was buried in St Oswald's Churchyard. His grave, which is much visited by tourists, is in a very pleasant location overlooking the riverside and the fells beyond.

Next to the Churchyard, by the rear entrance is the tiny, but famous, Sarah Nelson's Gingerbread Shop. Sarah Nelson was born in poverty in 1815 in Bowness. She went into service and eventually became a cook. She married a farm labourer, Wilfred Nelson and in 1850 they moved into Gate Cottage by the Church gate. This building had originally been the village school where William Wordsworth is known to have

**The path into Grasmere**

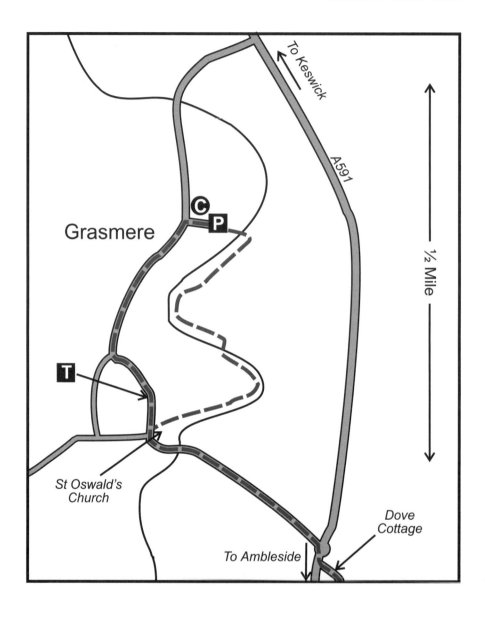

**Sarah Nelson's Gingerbread Shop**

taught. To make ends meet she took in washing and did some baking for Lady Farquhar who lived nearby. She learnt how to make gingerbread from Lady Farquhar's French chef and she sold it from her cottage to Victorian tourists. This venture was a great success and she became known as the 'Baker and Confectioner of Church Cottage, Grasmere'.

When she died in 1904 her recipe, which had been held in a local bank for safekeeping, passed to her great niece. The business has continued from the same shop ever since. The shop has remained unchanged since its days as the village school. Even the school coat pegs and the cupboard used to store the school slates remain in their original positions.

# 27. Rydal, White Moss

| | |
|---|---|
| **Distance:** | 1 mile there and back and a further 1½ miles on the roadside there and back |
| **Summary:** | This is a short woodland walk by the banks of the river Rothay which flows from Grasmere into Rydal Water. There are lovely views of the surrounding fells |
| **Car parking:** | Travelling from Ambleside to Grasmere, White Moss car park is situated on the left shortly after you pass the far end of Rydal Water. There are 2 disabled parking spaces |
| **Disabled toilet:** | On a path to the right about 100 yards after the start of the walk |
| **Path quality:** | Gradients are gentle and the path surface is quite good |
| **Map:** | Ordnance Survey Explorer OL7 Grid reference: NY352065 |

**The path down to the River Rothay**

**Rydal water from the roadside**

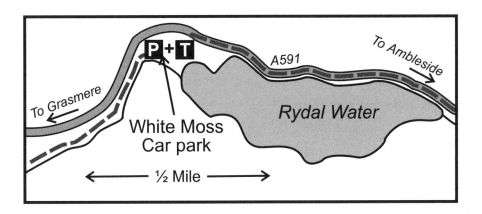

## Directions

The walk starts from the corner of the car park and continues straight on until a footbridge over the River Rothay is reached. Unfortunately this has steps and is inaccessible to wheelchairs but the path continues through a gate on the right across two more fields before becoming too steep and rough for wheelchairs. There is a pleasant riverside seat along here. Return is by the same route.

If you go back to the entrance of the car park and turn right there is a roadside path/pavement back along the shore of Rydal Water with stunning views across the lake. It is possible to follow this pavement all the way past the lake if you can endure the busy main road alongside.

# 28. Glenridding

**Distance:**   2 miles there and back

**Summary:**   A small but busy village, a beautiful and tranquil lake where Wordsworth saw his daffodils and a backdrop of dramatic hills — Glenridding has it all. Lake Ullswater is rightly thought by many to be amongst the most beautiful in the Lake District

**Car parking:** At the Ullswater Steamer terminal. There are 2 disabled parking spaces and a disabled toilet in the terminal building
Note: The main car park in Glenridding is on the left coming from Patterdale. It has 9 disabled parking spaces and a disabled toilet (RADAR key required). It is not advisable to use it however for this walk because there is not a suitable footpath along the main road to the start of the walk

**Disabled toilet:** On the approach road to the Steamers. There are 2 disabled parking spaces and a RADAR key is required

**Path quality:** Mainly level and smooth except for the track to Side Farm which is bumpy in places

**Map:**   Ordnance Survey Explorer OL5 Grid reference: NY390169

**The view from Side Farm**

# Directions

From the ferry terminal take the lakeside path through the field on the left signposted 'Howtown' and continue past the small boatyard to the road. Cross the road and follow the footpath, which is raised up along the side of the road. When the path rejoins the road, cross over and follow the 'permitted footpath' through some trees. Then cross over the road again, passing St. Patrick's Church on your right.

Immediately after the Church cross the road again at a dropped curb and continue carefully along the side of the road, without a pavement, for about 20 yards to reach a farm track on the left, down the side of the village hall and signposted by a rather concealed footpath sign to 'Howtown'. This track is rather bumpy at first but improves somewhat after the first cattle grid. It is necessary to use a gate into the field to avoid the cattle grid and this might well be too muddy in wet weather.

The gate round the second cattle grid presents no problems and beyond this the track rises fairly steeply and rather bumpily to Side Farm, where there is a tearoom. Through the farmyard the track goes left to Howtown and right to Hartsop. Both tracks are rather rough but it is worth taking the track to the right for about 100 yards and to look back across the valley towards Striding Edge. Return is by the same route.

## Points of interest

The Ullswater Steamers sail the length of the lake from Glenridding to Pooley Bridge, a journey of about an hour. There are disabled toilets in the terminal buildings at both Glenridding and Pooley Bridge, and one boat, The Lady Wakefield, even has a disabled toilet on board. If you do go to Pooley Bridge it is about ¼ of a mile from the pier to the village. Immediately before the bridge there is a car park on the left that leads to a short but pleasant riverside walk (about 200 yards each way). Back on the road there is no footpath over the bridge so great care is needed here.

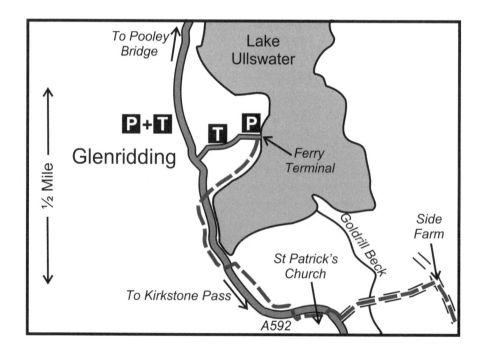

A mile north of Glenridding on the A592, Glencoyne Bay is the site of the daffodils, which are the subject of William Wordsworth's famous poem.

Glenridding is a popular starting point for hikers who wish to climb Helvellyn, the mountain seen across the valley from Side Farm. They often take the notorious Striding Edge route, which is a mile long knife-edge rock scramble along a narrow path along the top of precipitous crags. Helvellyn is a dangerous mountain, particularly in winter. The National Park Authority employs fell top assessors who climb Helvellyn every day in the Winter months to cheek on the weather and look out for such dangers as ice and unstable snow conditions. These are reported on the internet and in local shops and information centres so that walkers can plan their routes more safely.

# 29. Buttermere

| | |
|---|---|
| **Distance:** | 1¼ miles there and back |
| **Summary:** | Mountain views across the lake at every turn on this delightful lakeside walk. The view down the length of the lake, from point A is absolutely stunning |
| **Car parking:** | In Buttermere behind the Fish Hotel |
| **Disabled toilet:** | On the car park. RADAR key is required |
| **Path quality:** | Good surface of crushed stones, mainly level but with some short steeper sections |
| **Map:** | Ordnance Survey Explorer OL4 Grid reference: NY173169 |

## Directions

Go left from the entrance of the car park to pass in front of The Fish Hotel, and continue down the wide well surfaced track, through a couple of gates to reach the National Trust land near the lake. Take the right hand path along the side of the hedge, over the bridge and through the gate to join the lakeside path. After about ¾ mile a smaller path branches off to the left to avoid the uphill section of the main path. It is probably advisable to turn back at this point. There is steep up-hill and downhill ahead, with little in the way of views and then the path soon becomes inaccessible for wheelchairs.

## Points of interest

One of Buttermere's most famous residents was Mary Robinson who was a shepherdess and the daughter of the landlord of the Fish Inn. She became famous locally because she married the Hon. Alexander Hope M.P., brother of the Earl of Hopetoun, in 1802. She was known as 'The Beauty of Buttermere'. Unfortunately Alexander Hope was actually a bankrupt impostor called John Hatfield who had married her bigamously and he was hanged for forgery the following year. Mary later married a local farmer. William Wordsworth wrote about her at the time and more

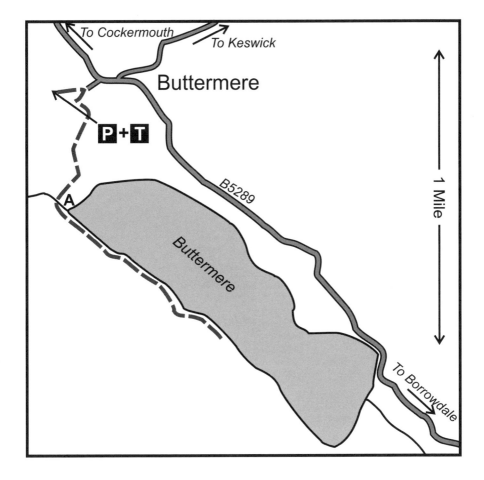

recently she became the subject of Melvin Bragg's novel *The Maid of Buttermere.*

The Church of St. James in Buttermere contains a memorial to the fell-walker and author Alfred Wainwright. It is situated in a window overlooking his favourite mountain Haystacks, where his ashes are scattered.

**The view down the lake**

# 30. Seathwaite

| | |
|---|---|
| **Distance:** | 2½ miles there and back |
| **Summary:** | This quiet cul-de-sac, through a lovely valley, leads to the footpath over Sty Head Pass to Wastdale Head at the very hub of the Lake District Mountains |
| **Car parking:** | On right of B5289 as you enter Seatoller from Keswick |
| **Disabled toilet:** | On car park. RADAR key required |
| **Path quality:** | Fairly quiet and fairly wide tarmac road with gentle gradients but no footpath |
| **Map:** | Ordnance Survey Explorer OL4 Grid reference: NY244138 |

## Directions

Turn left from the car park to go back down the road towards Keswick and take the first road on the right, signposted to Seathwaite. Follow this fairly quiet road for about a mile to the tiny hamlet of Seathwaite down a delightful small valley surrounded by steep-sided hills. Return is by the same route.

## Points of interest

Seathwaite is the wettest inhabited place in England with an annual rainfall of 140 inches. When we last visited it in October 2008 we could well believe it as many of the fields were waterlogged. This was nothing compared with the floods of September 1966 however when 5 inches of rain fell in one hour!

Seathwaite is a popular starting point for walkers wishing to climb Scafell Pike, Great Gable, and other mountains in the vicinity, as shown by the large number of cars which are invariably parked on its grass verges.

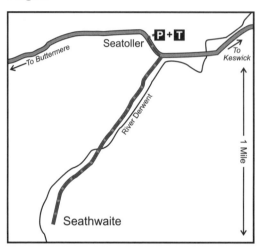

**The road looking towards Seathwaite**

# 31. Keswick, Whinlatter Forest

| | |
|---|---|
| **Distance:** | 1½ miles in total |
| **Summary**: | This is a very pleasant woodland walk with some open views of the surrounding hills. A map of way-marked trails can be bought from the Visitors Centre, but I have chosen the Revelin trail as being suitable for most wheelchair users |
| **Car parking:** | Turn left off the A66 Keswick to Cockermouth road at Braithwaite, a couple of miles or so from Keswick. Follow signs to the Whinlatter Forest visitor's centre, which is situated on the right of the road at the head of Whinlatter Pass. At the visitors centre follow the disabled signs up the incline to a car park behind the visitors centre where there are 3 disabled parking spaces |
| **Disabled toilet:** | Opposite the entrance to the shop |
| **Path quality:** | Fairly gentle gradients and fairly good surfaces throughout, except for a short section at point A. This section is narrow, uneven in places and has a poorly protected drop at one side |
| **Map**: | Ordnance Survey Explorer OL4 Grid reference: NY208245 |

## Directions

The Revelin trail starts from a car park about ¼ mile down the road from the visitors centre, so it is probably better to go by car. From the visitors centre turn left back down the road and the car park is up on your right after about ¼ mile. Follow the yellow way-marked signs. The path follows a woodland stream up a small valley, with benches at regular intervals for tired carers! The trees soon thin out with delightful views of the fells beyond. The path then crosses the stream and returns back down the hillside on a parallel track. After a further ¼ mile or so leave this track on a path to the right (yellow way-marked). This short path leads back to the stream and over a bridge (point A) to join the original path. (See note on path quality).

## Points of interest

Whinlatter forest was planted at the end of the First World War to counteract a shortage of timber at that time. It is England's only true mountain forest rising to an altitude of 2,591 feet at its highest point. The visitor centre has a range of displays relating to the forest including

**The path through the trees**

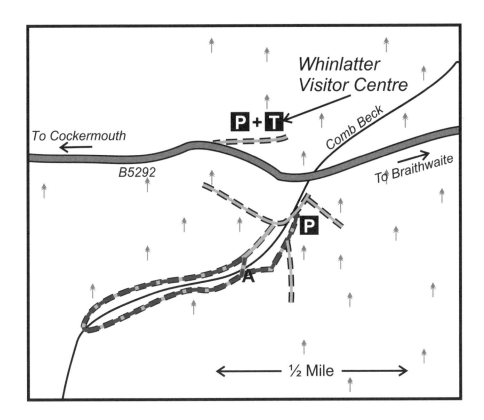

live CCTV pictures from the resident osprey nests. This can be seen whilst they raise their chicks from April to August. There is also a forest playground for children and forest trails for them starting from the visitor centre.

**The path at point A**

# 32. Keswick, Friar's Crag

| | |
|---|---|
| **Distance:** | 2 miles circular walk |
| **Summary:** | A lakeside and woodland walk to see this famous and popular beauty spot and viewpoint. There are picnic tables and seats overlooking the lake and the path along the road is separated from it by a hedge |
| **Car parking:** | Off the B5289, signposted to 'The Lake' at a roundabout as you leave Keswick. There are 6 disabled parking spaces |
| **Disabled toilet:** | On car park. RADAR key required |
| **Path quality:** | Good quality paths with mainly gentle gradients |
| **Map:** | Ordnance Survey Explorer OL4 Grid reference: NY264228 |

## Directions

From the car park turn left along the road and continue along the side of the lake, to where the path divides. The path continues to the left, with a disabled sign pointing the way (point A), but it is well worth going straight on here for the spectacular view down the lake from Frair's Crag. Returning to point A, the path descends to the lakeshore and then enters woodland before reaching a farm track. Turn left here up to the road, and take the path to the left, alongside the road and behind a hedge. After about ½ mile take the narrow path at right angles away from the road to the left, between a hedge and a fence. This path leads into the woods and back to the car park.

**The view from Friar's Crag**

**Hope Park looking towards Keswick**

## Points of interest

Hope Park, opposite the car park is a delightful municipal park with impressive views over Keswick to the fells beyond. Paths are of fairly level tarmac. The park was originally a miniature golf course and ornamental gardens belonging to Sir Percy and Lady Hope. It was opened to the public in 1927 and taken over by the town council in 1974. Today its attractions include ornamental gardens, a woodland walk, miniature golf courses and a plant centre. It is very popular, being situated on the the route of a stroll from the town centre to the lake and has the magnificent lakeland scenery as a backdrop.

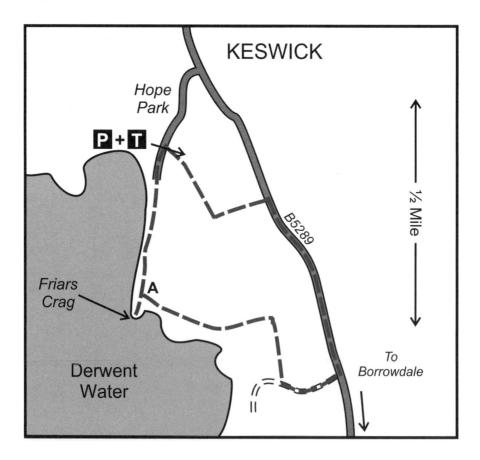

# 33. Threlkeld

| | |
|---|---|
| **Distance:** | 3 miles in total |
| **Summary:** | An interesting and pleasant walk along the old railway track and by the side of the River Greta. The section between B and C is really only suitable for powered wheelchairs and scooters because of the gradient and the gradient at A would require a strong pusher for manual wheelchair users. |
| **Car parking:** | Turn left off the A66 from Keswick, signposted 'Threlkeld'. After about ¼ mile the car park is signposted to the right |
| **Disabled toilet:** | On the car park. RADAR key is required |
| **Path quality:** | There is a fairly steep slope down to the railway track at point A and then the path is level with a good surface until point B. The road between B and C rises very steeply, then it is a gentle descent along a narrow country lane, with some traffic, back to Threlkeld |
| **Map:** | Ordnance Survey Explorer OL5 Grid reference: NY323254 |

## Directions

Turn left out of the car park and retrace your route back to the A66, taking care as there is no footpath for much of the way. At the main road the footpath to the right leads, after a few yards, down a steep incline to

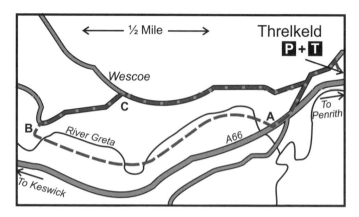

the bed of the old Cockermouth to Penrith railway. This travels besides the River Greta through a pleasant wooded valley. It crosses the river two or three times on impressive bridges of arched ironwork and also burrows underground two or three times through equally impressive short tunnels. There are a couple of stone shelters along this section of the railway with information boards about the old railway, and opposite the second one take a short field path on the right, leaving the railway to join a minor road. Turn right and continue steeply uphill for about ¼ mile to the hamlet of Wescoe. Turn right at the top of the hill and follow the lane back to Threlkeld.

**The hamlet of Wescoe**

# 34. Borrowdale, The Bowder Stone

| | |
|---|---|
| **Distance:** | ³/₄ mile there and back |
| **Summary:** | A wooded walk through difficult terrain to see a truly amazing rock formation. The path passes an old fenced-off quarry used nowadays for abseiling practice — rather them than me! |
| **Car parking:** | On left of B5289 about 5 miles from Keswick. Disabled parking is allowed in the bus lay-by just past the car park entrance |
| **Disabled toilet:** | On the car park at Rosthwaite 1¹/₂ miles away |
| **Path quality:** | Steep in places, reasonably good pebbly surface |
| **Map:** | Ordnance Survey Explorer OL4 Grid reference: NY253168 |

## Directions

The path rises up steeply for a considerable distance from the bus lay-by and then levels out somewhat after a gate until the Bowder Stone is reached. There are glimpses of the River Derwent through the trees, down to the right along this section. The path continues on past the Bowder Stone but it is too rough for wheelchairs beyond this point.

## Points of interest

The Bowder Stone is 30 feet high and weighs some 2000 tons. It is not a local rock however and was probably brought down from Scotland by glacial action and deposited in its present incredible position in the last Ice Age.

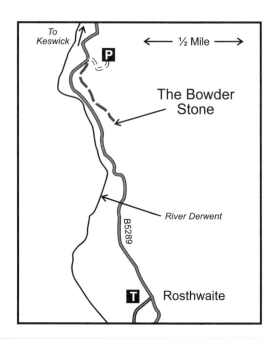

**The Bowder Stone**

# 35. Keswick Railway Station

| | |
|---|---|
| **Distance:** | Up to 8 miles there and back |
| **Summary:** | This walk, with exceptional views of the River Greta follows the track of the old railway for four miles all the way to Threlkeld, joining up with walk 33 which starts from the other end |
| **Car parking:** | Travelling west on the A66 take the A5271 towards Keswick (first exit off the roundabout) and after a short distance turn left by the garage, signposted 'Leisure Pool and Fitness Centre'. After about ¾ mile turn right at the roundabout and then immediately left to park in the parking bays in front of the Station. Note that the first three parking bays are reserved for customers of the Leisure Pool and Fitness Centre |
| **Disabled toilet:** | At the Railway Station at the start of the walk. RADAR key is required |
| **Path quality:** | Fairly good surface and gentle gradients except for a large hill as you leave Keswick |
| **Map:** | Ordnance Survey Explorer OL4 Grid reference: NY272238 |

## Directions

Starting from the railway station the route soon crosses the River Greta and the road from Grasmere on a fine bridge and then continues on an embankment at roof top level, through the outskirts of Keswick. The path then rises up through an embankment to go under a large concrete

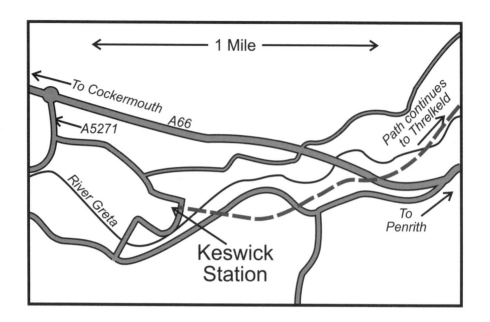

bridge, which carries the A66 Keswick bypass. It is not clear on the ground just where the path leaves the original railway track to accommodate the building of the new bridge, but it obviously does so because just beyond the bridge there is a spectacular boardwalk section, which clings to the wooded slopes high above the River Greta. The path then descends to the original bed of the old railway and continues along the valley towards Threlkeld.

## Points of interest

The Cockermouth, Keswick and Penrith Railway was opened in 1865 to connect the iron works of West Cumbria around Workington with those of the North East around Durham, via the existing railway networks of the time. It carried mining materials and passengers until its closure in 1972.

In its heyday Keswick Station was far more extensive than the single building and platform that survives today. There were three platforms connected by an underpass, a goods yard and a turntable. The Railway

Company offices were also located at the station and they built and owned the adjacent Keswick Hotel.

In recent years there has been a proposal to re-open the route with a modern railway but at an estimated cost, which currently stands in the region of £100 million pounds, it seems far from likely that the project will ever go ahead.

**Keswick Railway Station**

# 36. Mungrisdale

| | |
|---|---|
| **Distance:** | 6 miles there and back |
| **Summary:** | A pleasant walk along a country lane which is quiet and peaceful until you get near to the busy A66. There are some long distance views across the surrounding countryside |
| **Car parking:** | Lay-by opposite the Recreation Rooms in Mungrisdale |
| **Disabled toilet:** | Nearest one 5 miles away at Threlkeld |
| **Path quality:** | Tarmac road throughout with some steep sections. There are several gates to open and close along the way |
| **Map:** | Ordnance Survey Explorer OL5 Grid reference: NY364303 |

**The gated road looking towards Mungrisdale**

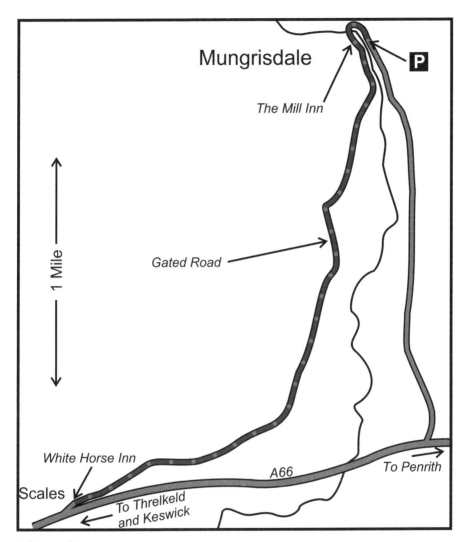

## Directions

From the lay-by in Mungrisdale continue up the road and take the first left over the bridge and immediately left again to continue on past the Mill Inn. The walk continues straight on along the gated road until you reach the White Horse Inn in the village of Scales. Return is by the same route.

# Also from Sigma Leisure:

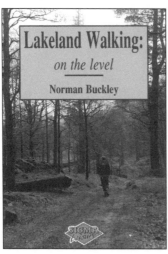